PELICAN BOOKS

The Anglo-Saxons

David M. Wilson is Professor of Medieval Archaeology at
London University and is a past president of the British
Archaeological Association and of the Viking Society
for Northern Research. He has written a number
of books including *A Catalogue of Anglo-Saxon
Ornamental Metalwork, 700–1100, in the British
Museum, Viking Art* (with O. Klindt-Jensen) and
The Viking Achievement (with P. G. Foote).
He is a corresponding member of the German
Archaeological Institute and of the Royal Gustav Adolf's
Academy of Sweden. He is married to a book-illustrator,
has two children, and spends as much time as possible
in his Manx cottage.

DAVID WILSON

The Anglo-Saxons

PENGUIN BOOKS

Penguin Books Ltd, Harmondsworth, Middlesex, England
Penguin Books Australia Ltd, Ringwood, Victoria, Australia
Penguin Books Canada Ltd, 41 Steelcase Road West,
Markham, Ontario, Canada
Penguin Books (N.Z.) Ltd, 182–190 Wairau Road,
Auckland 10, New Zealand

First published as a volume in the 'Ancient Peoples and Places'
series, edited by Glyn Daniel, by Thames & Hudson 1960
Revised edition first published in Pelican Books 1971
Reprinted 1972, 1975
Copyright © Thames & Hudson, 1966

Made and printed in Great Britain by
Hazell Watson & Viney Ltd, Aylesbury, Bucks
Set in Linotype Granjon

Contents

LIST OF FIGURES   7

LIST OF PLATES   8

FOREWORD   11

FOREWORD TO THE SECOND EDITION   12

INTRODUCTION: THE STUDY OF ANGLO-SAXON
    ARCHAEOLOGY   13

1. HISTORICAL BACKGROUND AND
    PAGAN BURIALS   25

2. CHRISTIAN ANTIQUITIES   48

3. THE LIFE OF THE PEOPLE   63

4. WEAPONS AND WARFARE   108

5. ANGLO-SAXON ART   131

BOOK LIST   159

SOURCES OF ILLUSTRATIONS   163

NOTES ON THE PLATES   165

INDEX   175

FIGURES

1. Montelius's railway carriages, p 14
2. Map: Kingdoms and peoples of Anglo-Saxon England, p. 28
3. Boars from Sutton Hoos claps, p. 44
4. Standard from Sutton Hoo, p. 45
5. SS. Peter and Paul, Canterbury, plan, p. 50
6. Architectural details from Anglo-Saxon churches, p. 52
7. The Gandersheim casket, p. 59
8. Reconstructions of Anglo-Saxon houses, p. 72
9. Plans of Anglo-Saxon houses, pp. 74-5
10a, b. Plough and harrow (Bayeux Tapestry), pp. 76-7
11. Tools from Hurbuck, Co. Durham, pp. 78-9
12. Implements from late Anglo-Saxon MSS., p. 80
13. Man using a spade (Bayeux Tapestry), p. 81
14. Implements from Sandtun, Kent, p. 81
15. *Relief-band amphora* from the Rhineland, p. 88
16. Men drawing a barrel on a cart (Bayeux Tapestry), p. 90
17. The Sutton Hoo ship, p 91
18. Clothes from eleventh century MSS., p. 93
19. Three small long-brooches, p. 96
20. Anglo-Saxon pottery, p. 101
21. Anglo-Saxon pottery, p. 103
22. Anglo-Saxon glassware, p. 105
23. Sword hilts, pp. 110-11
24. Warrior, from late Saxon MS., p. 114
25. Reconstructed Anglo-Saxon shield, p. 116
26. Shields and weapons from Anglo-Saxon MSS., p. 117
27. Anglo-Saxon spearheads from London, p. 119
28. *Francisca* from Howletts, Kent, p. 121
29. Transporting weapons (Bayeux Tapestry), p. 124
30. Warrior (Bayeux Tapestry), p. 125

31. Early Anglo-Saxon animal ornament, p. 134
32. Ribbon-style ornament, p. 135
33. Animal ornament from the Witham pins, p. 140
34. Ornament on gold ring from Poslingford, p. 141
35. Animal ornament from Trewhiddle, p. 142
36. German, Irish and English animal ornament, p. 143
37. Stone cross from Middleton, Yorks., p. 155
38. Animal ornament on tenth-century shrine, p. 157

PLATES

1. Jewelled clasp from Sutton Hoo
2. Dismantled jewelled mounts from the Sutton Hoo sword
3. Two silver dishes from Sutton Hoo
4. Jewelled gold buckle from Sutton Hoo
5. Jewelled gold strap-distributor from Sutton Hoo
6. Jewelled gold buckle from Sutton Hoo
7. The great gold buckle from Sutton Hoo
8. The Sutton Hoo helmet
9. The Sutton Hoo purse-lid
10. Terminal of the Sutton Hoo whetstone
11. Fish from a Sutton Hoo hanging-bowl
12. Tower of Earls Barton church, Northants.
13. Interior of Escomb church, Co. Durham
14. Apse of Wing church, Bucks.
15. Church of St Lawrence, Bradford-on-Avon, Wilts.
16. Silver-mounted portable altar
17. The Trewhiddle chalice
18. Plates from a house-shaped shrine
19. Anglo-Saxon silver pennies
20. Group of cruciform brooches
21. Group of saucer brooches
22. The Abingdon sword
23. The Witham sword
24. The Fetter Lane sword pommel
25. Fragment of a leather scabbard from Hexham, Northumberland
26. *Scramasax* from Sittingbourne, Kent
27. *Scramasax* from Winchester
28. Boar from the Benty Grange helmet
29. The Benty Grange helmet

30. Buckle from Worms, Germany
31. Buckle from Kent (?)
32. Buckle from Smithfield
33. Necklace from Desborough, Northants.
34. The Haslingfield equal-armed brooch
35. The Kingston Brooch
36. Jewelled brooch from Breach Down, Kent
37. Jewelled brooch from Faversham, Kent
38. Jewelled pendant from Faversham, Kent
39. The Wynaldum buckle-plate
40. St Cuthbert's pectoral cross
41. The Ixworth cross
42. The Wilton cross
43. The Middleton Moor hanging-bowl escutcheons
44. Buckle and clasps from Taplow, Bucks.
45. The Winchester hanging-bowl
46. Symbol from the Book of Durrow
47. The Ezra folio from the Codex Amiatinus
48. Carpet page from the Lindisfarne Gospels
49. Evangelist portrait from the Lindisfarne Gospels
50. Evangelist symbol from the Echternach Gospels
51. Evangelist portrait from the St Chad Gospels
52. Page of canon tables from MS. Royal 1.E VI
53. The Ruthwell cross
54. Figure of Christ, from the lid of St Cuthbert's coffin
55. The Witham pins
56. The Franks Casket
57. The Alfred Jewel
58. The back of the Alfred Jewel
59. The Minster Lovell Jewel
60. The Dowgate Hill brooch
61. The Tassilo Chalice
62. The Kirkoswald brooch
63. Part of the Trewhiddle hoard
64. The Strickland brooch
65. The Fuller brooch
66. Cross head from Cropthorne, Worcs.
67. Trial-piece of bone from York
68. St Cuthbert's stole
69. The Annunciation from the Benedictional of St Aethelwold
70. The donation folio from the Charter of the New Minster, Winchester

71. Scene from MS., British Museum, Harley 603
72. Sculptured stones at Bakewell, Derbyshire
73. Angel from the church of St Lawrence, Bradford-on-Avon, Wiltshire
74. Viking gravestone from St Paul's churchyard, London
75. Ivory panel from Winchester
76. Ivory comb in the British Museum
77. Reverse side of the same comb
78. The Sutton, Isle of Ely, disc brooch
79. Censer cover from Canterbury

Foreword

THIS book is intended to give a general view of Anglo-Saxon culture as seen through the eyes of the archaeologist. No book of this length can hope to do more than sketch the broad outlines of the subject; consequently I have had to be selective in my approach and I am only too conscious of the many gaps that occur in this story of six hundred years of the most formative period of English history.

It would be impossible to give separate acknowledgements for all the help I have received during the writing of this book, but I cannot allow it to go to press without some indication of my indebtedness. My thanks are due to Mr G. Ashburner for providing me with so many brilliant photographs. I am grateful to Professor Holger Arbman, Mrs S. Hawkes, Dr Ole Klindt-Jensen and Mrs M. Saunders for long hours of discussion of the problems of Anglo-Saxon archaeology. The day-to-day contact with my colleagues in the British Museum has provoked discussion, which has naturally influenced my thoughts on the subject, and my debt to them, and to the institution itself, cannot be sufficiently acknowledged. I would particularly like to thank Mr Julian Brown, who has allowed me to read, before publication, his revolutionary theories concerning the Lindisfarne Gospels, and Mr R. H. M. Dolley who, over a number of years, has patiently answered many questions on numismatic subjects. Mr Rupert Bruce-Mitford and Mr Peter Lasko kindly read the typescript of this book and offered me much advice and help which I deeply appreciate. I must thank the editors of *Arms and Armour* for the use of the translations of the passage of poetry on p. 102.

Dr Glyn Daniel's encouragement and advice has helped me

enormously and must be acknowledged here. I must thank my mother for her patience in reading through the typescript and putting in the commas. My wife has helped me immeasurably, with criticism, with typing and, above all, with her drawings — for she has drawn all but one of the line illustrations.

D.M.W.

FOREWORD TO THE SECOND EDITION

It is ten years since this book was first published and in that time the subject has developed and expanded considerably. The book I wrote ten years ago is now out of date and I have attempted in this new edition to cover the discoveries and theories unveiled since then. Large portions of the introduction and of chapters 2 and 3 have been completely re-written and a number of new text figures have replaced illustrations now out-dated. I must once again thank my wife for her drawings and for reading the revised edition in proof.

D.M.W.

The Study of Anglo-Saxon Archaeology

At the end of the nineteenth century archaeology had emerged from the antiquarianism of the early Victorian period, and from the quarrels attendant on the evolutionary theories, into a rigid discipline based on two methods of study – excavation and typology. General Pitt-Rivers had reduced excavation to a science, carried out with military precision, and had inculcated into the minds of the hitherto rather lackadaisical field archaeologist a belief in scientific accuracy. It was many years, however, before English archaeologists had learnt the lessons he taught and reached the standard of thoroughness that has placed English field archaeology in its present pre-eminent position. The second method of study was developed in England by Sir John Evans and Pitt-Rivers, and in Scandinavia by Oscar Montelius and his disciple Bernhard Salin. A close and detailed study of the material remains of ancient people produced a system of 'typology'. The basis of typology is the fact that manufactured objects are subject to evolutionary processes. Sometimes the evolution can be seen as a gradual improvement in form or function, or both; occasionally it can only be seen as a development in decoration. This is best illustrated by Montelius's own example of the development of the railway carriage [Fig. 1]. Starting as a horse-drawn coach, adapted to run on rails, it developed in form through various stages: first as three combined coaches made into one carriage until in the late nineteenth century the only trace of its coaching ancestry was to be seen in the curved bottoms of the side windows of the first-class compartments. Typology can be used for its own sake or applied chronologically. A typological

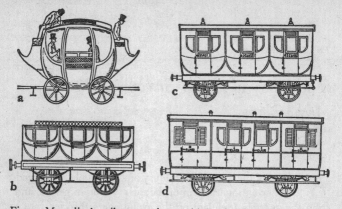

Fig. 1. Montelius's railway carriages: (a) England 1825; (b) Austria 1840; (c) and (d) Sweden/Germany c. 1850

sequence showing, say, the development of the form of a particular type of brooch can then be used as a scale against which chronological judgements can be made. Thus an object found with a brooch of typologically early form might be said to be, in all probability, earlier in date than an object found with a brooch of the same group, but of a more developed form. The archaeologist calls this 'dating by association'.

The two methods outlined above, together with the examination of standing monuments, have provided the basis for the archaeological study of the Anglo-Saxon period. The natural scientist has developed technical devices to help the archaeologist, some of which have been applied to this period. But the resistivity survey of an area prior to excavation and the radiocarbon method of dating organic materials must be seen not as developments of method but as developments of technique – logical extensions of techniques developed over the last hundred years.

By a study of the material remains of man and by the study of man's effect on his environment the archaeologist aims at a reconstruction of man's past behaviour. To a great extent his study results in a catalogue of the externals of man's life in a given period, his economic and material behaviour; it results in a catalogue of the features of houses, dress, agricultural systems, trade and technical achievement, set as far as possible in a chronological sequence. It is difficult – almost impossible – for an archaeologist to reconstruct man's mental processes from the archaeological evidence alone, and to this extent the Anglo-Saxon archaeologist is lucky in that he deals with a period for which historical sources are available. At times these sources are meagre, but they do give a reasonably clear view of the social and economic structure of the society and of the beliefs, customs and law of the English in this period.

By collaboration, the archaeologist and historian can enlarge each other's experience as is illustrated by the result of the excavations at the site of a royal township at Yeavering in Northumberland. There can be no doubt that this site is *ad Gefrin*, the royal township mentioned by Bede as the place to which Paulinus went, with King Edwin, in 627 to preach Christianity to the people of Bernicia. The site is discussed in greater detail in a later chapter (pp. 64f.), but it may not be out of place here to mention how, in the investigation of this site, archaeologists have helped historians and, conversely, how historians have helped archaeologists. The archaeologist provided for the historian, among other facts, some idea of the physical appearance of a Saxon royal township, the ground-plan and probable reconstruction of the meeting place of a moot and a rough date for the abandonment of the site. The historian provided for the archaeologist the identity of the site, a knowledge of the likely purposes of the various buildings and a fixed date in a sequence of relative dates.

Such cooperation has not always been so happy, but scholars from both disciplines have learnt to consult with each other and with their colleagues in related fields – place names, geography and botany, to mention but a few. In a book which attempts to present a brief view of Anglo-Saxon England on the basis of the archaeological material I shall be using evidence from many disciplines; but as this is primarily an archaeological study the limits of the archaeological evidence must be defined. This essay will not reveal to us the sense of humour, the philosophy, the social customs or sexual morality of the Anglo-Saxon people. It will not even tell us a great deal about chieftainship, slavery or middle-class respectability, although by intuitive guesses and out of human experience we can reach some way towards these things by examining burial customs, the wealth of graves, the size of buildings or cases of human sacrifice. The heroic character of the Anglo-Saxons, so clearly portrayed in their imaginative literature and poetry, is only dimly perceived in their material remains, and archaeologists must admit that their material only illuminates some of the more mundane elements of the period.

Our evidence lies largely in the economic field. From excavation of graves and settlement sites the externals of life become clearer. Houses have been excavated in great numbers in the last few years and, although we cannot yet generalize for the whole country, we are beginning to understand a little of the appearance of Anglo-Saxon settlement sites. This is especially so since excavations at Mucking, Essex, and West Stow, Suffolk, have at last started to yield a picture of village life in the early Anglo-Saxon period. From excavation of settlement sites we are beginning to learn a little about food: examination of animal bones tells of the domestic and wild animals eaten by the villagers and botanical analysis tells of the grain grown in the fields. Our knowledge of Anglo-Saxon agricultural practices is slight, but a good deal of attention is being paid to this aspect of the economy and we may soon learn something about the fields and enclosures of the period.

Industrial processes have been more thoroughly documented in the last few years. Excavations of a series of kiln sites has added to our knowledge of the pottery industry. The metalworker, the weaver and the miller are all gradually yielding their secrets to the archaeologist's spade, and even the carpenter has left some traces. But the glass-maker, the basket-maker, the bone-worker and one or two other industries have left only their products, and no remnants of their tools or workshops.

Although a fair amount is known about weaving there is little information about clothes and, although a great deal of jewellery survives, we know little of fashion. Combs are common, but there is little evidence about hairdressing. Dice and gaming pieces tell of indoor games which are often difficult to reconstruct, as is the music which was played on the remaining fragmentary instruments. We have clues about trade – we have a great number of coins for instance – but information about transport is slight. From such a patchwork we must reconstruct our picture of Anglo-Saxon society; but in some respects our picture is more complete.

Our knowledge of warfare, of which there is a great deal of contemporary literary evidence, is illuminated by military earthworks and by the large number of surviving weapons. The decorative arts are well represented and the artists' products still tease the eye. Christianity has left abundant remains – churches, vestments, liturgical equipment and stone crosses – and excavation at Winchester has now revealed the outline of one of the greatest of all English cathedral complexes.

Although knowledge of the material world increases year by year it must be pointed out that the period of study is a long one – 650 years. Although it is possible to generalize on the basis of our few finds we must recognize that in these twenty-six generations tastes and practices changed considerably. Changes can be clearly seen in such objects as pots and brooches but they are by no means so clear when one considers the forms of houses, fortifications, or settlements. For this reason the erecting of a chronological scheme is one of the most important exercises of the Anglo-Saxon archaeologist, for only thus can he set his material in a historical context.

As yet natural scientific methods, such as radio-carbon dating and dendrochronology, have not materially helped the Anglo-Saxon archaeologist who must still rely on typological dating for much of his chronological framework. This method of building up a relative chronology is best expressed by an adaptation of a 'formula' first expressed by Montelius. An object A found with an object B $(A+B)$ is dated by reference to an object, E, of known date through the link: $A+B = B+C = C+D = D+E$, each stage in the formula representing a different archaeological find. In such a case the margin of uncertainty must grow with every link until even relative dating statements are meaningless. It is clear that such a method must be used with great caution and cannot be counted accurate, although the temptation to place archaeological material together with a historical event has sometimes proved overwhelming to the student of the Anglo-Saxon period. The archaeological method is useful in providing a broad chronology against which material may be set, but its use in making fine historical judgements is indefensible.

It might be thought that, where a large number of objects are involved, dating by these methods might be more reliable. Professor Bertil Almgren, however, has shown statistically, by means of a study of the largest group of Viking brooches found in Scandinavia, that objects found in association with any individual brooch cannot be dated to within a century. The same reasoning is true of the whole of the pagan Anglo-Saxon period. In the late Anglo-Saxon period, however, it is possible to date certain objects, and particularly metalwork, more closely. First, a few objects can be dated because they are inscribed with the names of known historical figures; secondly, certain objects are found with coin hoards, which can now be dated with extreme accuracy; and, thirdly, certain objects are known to have belonged to historical people, having been found, for example, in their coffins. The table opposite shows all the pieces of late Saxon ornamental metalwork found in such contexts.

It can be seen from this table that while there is a certain amount of dating evidence for the ninth and eleventh centuries, the evidence for the eighth and tenth centuries is practically non-existent. Even with these accurately dated parallels, few scholars would dare to date a piece of ornamental Anglo-Saxon metalwork of this period to within a century, even with the help of the contemporary illuminated manuscripts. How very much more difficult to date the featureless axe or spearhead! More fragile objects can perhaps be more closely dated by coin evidence. It happens occasionally, as at Chester and Morley St Peter in Norfolk, that a hoard of coins is hidden in a pot. Such an object, because it is cheap and easily broken, may not have been of any great antiquity when it was buried, and the date of its manufacture can probably be placed within a few years of its deposition; but there are not many such pots. Precious objects, however, have a tendency to be handed down from one generation to another, as was the sword mentioned in 1015 in a will of the Atheling Æthelstan: 'to my brother Edmund I grant the sword

Datable Ornamental Metalwork of the Late Anglo-Saxon Period

Cent-ury	Personal Dating	Objects associated with the burials of Historical Persons	Objects found in Coin Hoards
7th		Certain objects from the coffin of St Cuthbert (*d.* 687)	Sutton Hoo (*c.* 650–60) Crondall (*c.* 670)
8th	The Tassilo Chalice (777–88) (made in Germany under strong English influence)		
9th	K. Æthelwulf's ring (836–67) Q. Æthelswith's ring (855–89) Bp Æthilwald's seal (*c.* 850) The Alfred Jewel (871–99)		Sevington (*c.* 850) Hexham (*c.* 850) Hon, Norway (*c.* 855) Kirkoswald (*c.* 855) Gravesend (*c.* 872) Beeston Tor (*c.* 875) Trewhiddle (*c.* 872–5) Talnotrie (*c.* 900)
10th			Cuerdale (*c.* 903–5)
11th		Pin of Abp. Wulfstan of York (1002–1023) *King Edward the Confessor's Cross* (1042–66) (*lost*)	Igelösa, Sweden (*c.* 1005) Stockholm, Sweden (*c.* 1025) Sutton, Isle of Ely (*c.* 1066–87) *St Mary at Hill* (*c.* 1075) (*lost*)

which belonged to King Offa'. The sword was more than two hundred and twenty years old when the prince died! On a humbler scale can be mentioned the case quoted by Mr Lethbridge of a ten-year-old girl, 'who was buried with brooches, girdle hangers and other things, which were worn or patched at the time of burial. She was provided with festoons of beads much too big for her. She was not buried with her own jewels, but with old and worn-out objects, which had probably belonged to her mother. They had been picked out of some old remnants chest. The cracked brooch with its missing garnets, the girdle hangers roughly patched for the occasion – these may have belonged once to her grandmother or great-aunt.'

This problem of absolute dating has exercised all who have written about Anglo-Saxon archaeology. Baldwin-Brown for instance, in the early years of this century, evolved a cypher by means of which he divided up each century into thirds, assigning archaeological materials to one of these short periods. In the later years of his life, E. T. Leeds would often bend over backwards in an attempt to avoid too accurate a dating statement. In this book I must follow the example of Leeds: where a definite dating statement is made, it is made with all due qualifications; a book bristling with 'probably' and 'possibly' would make tedious reading: the reader must supply his own qualifications.

The Anglo-Saxon archaeologist must admit that his chronology is one of the weaker points in the present state of his subject's growth. Once this is admitted, a thorough study of the material can lead him to make historical judgements of a much broader type than those made by his predecessors. His material can be interpreted in its economic and social setting; he can make judgements about trade and kingship, about diet and about craftsmanship which were impossible fifty years ago. The time will come when a relative chronology can be erected for the whole of the Anglo-Saxon period on a basis acceptable to both the statistician and the historian. With the aid of new scientific methods, such as dendrochronology (tree-ring dating) and radiocarbon dating techniques, it may even be possible within the next fifty years to build up a reasonably accurate absolute chronology. We are not yet in this happy state, however, and, until we are, the Anglo-Saxon archaeologist must be wary of making historical judgements which have fine chronological implications.

Once such limitations are realized the archaeologist can help the historian and one might instance the study of trade. Nearly thirty-five years ago the greatest of all Anglo-Saxon historians, Sir Frank Stenton, wrote, 'The beginnings of English foreign trade lie in an obscurity which is only broken by occasional grants of freedom from toll to monasteries owning sea-going ships, by discoveries of early English coins on the Continent and by incidental references to trade or traders in ecclesiastical narratives.' Like others, archaeologists and historians, before him, he did not use the archaeological evidence, which tells of trading connexions in luxury goods long before written evidence appears. European archaeology abounds in such evidence: Frankish glass, perhaps made on the Rhine, is found in Wales, Eastern Mediterranean pottery is found in Cornwall, and Byzantine silver in Suffolk. Rich silks from the East found in St Cuthbert's coffin are an indication of a considerable trade in such materials at an earlier period, while bronze bowls from Coptic Egypt, ivory from Africa and cowrie shells from tropical waters found in Anglo-Saxon graves tell of far-flung trading connexions in the period before England had become Christian. In the later period Anglo-Saxon swords are found in Norway and Anglo-Saxon coins occur in Polish hoards, Norwegian hones are found in London, while fragments of German stone mortars are found at Thetford. These material remains tell us as much of the direction and scope of the trade of Anglo-Saxon England as all the documents that the historian can produce. Dr G. C. Dunning, for example, has traced, by means of archaeological material, the changing currents of the cross-Channel wine trade, reinforcing historical evidence with material facts and filling in certain gaps in the historian's knowledge.

One particular branch of the study of the Anglo-Saxon period has developed by leaps and bounds in recent years. Investigation by such scholars as Mr Grierson, Mr Dolley and Mr Blunt of the problem of the Anglo-Saxon coinage have resolved many archaeological and historical problems. Problems of minting and moneying, of circulation and coinage reform have been answered, mainly by a re-examination of material already in collectors' trays. The body of numismatic evidence is so great that most new finds serve mainly to confirm the results of the re-examination of the material. For the first time since the late nineteenth century, the problem of the decorative style of the Anglo-Saxon coinage has been tackled logically. For instance, Mr Dolley, in a thorough study of certain later coins of Æthelred II (979–1013), identified nine 'styles', each one distinguished by a different form of bust on the reverse of the coin. Each style is regional and has been given a geographical label – Northern, Southern, Eastern, etc. The historical implications of this have been followed up by Mr Dolley who has suggested that the reason for the regional stylistic distinction at this stage of Æthelred's reign, where it had not occurred before, was a deliberate decentralization in the face of the great Danish attacks which culminated in Canute's conquest of the country. Such a conclusion can and does lead to other historical judgements which are of deep significance.

Numismatic judgements can similarly have great significance in relation to the archaeological material. Edgar's sexennial cycle of coin types, by which a new type of coin was issued every six years and the coins in circulation called in, has been recognized by the numismatist in the structure of the coin hoards of the tenth and eleventh centuries. The archaeological implications of the dating of hoards to within six years or less in the late Anglo-Saxon period are of great importance and not yet fully appreciated.

From the work of the numismatist the Anglo-Saxon archaeologist can learn a lesson, for the methods of study are often very similar. The Anglo-Saxon archaeologist's material has been collected over a couple of centuries, mainly from graves and hoards or found casually in isolation. It is common for a research student to take a group of these objects, the small long-brooches, for example, and study them, erect a typological structure based on his study, discuss its origin and degenerations and make a few remarks on its geographical distribution. All this is very valuable work and one of the great aims of the future Anglo-Saxon archaeologist must be to publish all the material lying neglected in museums up and down the country. But Anglo-Saxon archaeologists have never tackled problems which seem to me to be equally useful and interesting. Mr Jessup has discussed in detail the methods of manufacture of the Kentish garnet jewellery, but nobody has yet discussed the technical aspects of the structure of the Anglo-Saxon shield. Except in the cases of individual cemeteries, nobody has yet bothered to examine the skeletons found in Anglo-Saxon graves for evidence of longevity, disease or diet, although some work is now in train on the dental evidence. Nobody has yet collected the evidence available in the Anglo-Saxon archaeological material for fishing, agriculture and similar pursuits. Many publications of Anglo-Saxon cemeteries contain short reports on the impressions of cloth rusted on the buckle plates or shield bosses, but nobody has yet gone round looking at every single example of impressed cloth structure on metal objects, although Mrs Crowfoot made a gallant beginning. Nobody in modern times has investigated thoroughly the interesting problems of dress and fashion in the period. All these are problems, typical of hundreds that could be listed, which could be worked on and discussed in the present stage of our knowledge.

By the detailed re-examination of the material remains, new facts are bound to emerge. The articles of Mr Jackson and Sir Eric Fletcher on various aspects of Anglo-Saxon architecture demonstrate, most clearly, how such a re-examination can add to our appreciation of the period. Their re-appraisal of the Anglo-Saxon church at Lydd, for instance, has shown conclusively that this church must be one of the earliest in England and that it may date from the pre-Augustinian era. Their conclusions were reached by merely looking at the church in detail, with their minds completely free from preconceived ideas as to its structure.

Anglo-Saxon archaeology until the 1939–45 war was very largely a 'museum' study; the student examined objects in museums or excavated cemeteries, and then studied his finds in association with other objects in the same grave, and in relation to similar objects discovered elsewhere. Since the war, however, he has turned his attention much more to field work. We have already mentioned the excavations at Yeavering carried out by Mr Hope-Taylor: to these can be added Group Captain Knocker's and (more recently) Mr Davison's excavations on the site of the Anglo-Saxon town of Thetford, Sir Cyril Fox's classic study of Offa's Dyke, the great linear earthwork which stretched along the border of Wales and Mercia, Mr Rahtz's excavations at the rich farm of Cheddar, Miss Cramp's excavations of the site of Bede's monastery at Monkwearmouth, Mr Hope-Taylor's excavation of the royal manor at Old Windsor, and Mr Biddle's investigations of the early minsters at Winchester. These have initiated a programme of investigations of sites other than cemeteries which will continue to broaden our basic knowledge of Anglo-Saxon culture. What is more interesting is that the archaeologist has been working together with the historian on all these sites. In the words of Professor Grimes, 'The day is past when the historian, the philologist, the art historian and the archaeologist could ignore each other – not perhaps with impunity (for this was never so), but without attracting adverse criticism for such action. Today all four disciplines, and many others too, including the more purely scientific ones, must work together more closely if they are to make significant progress.'

In this book I have attempted to combine with the evidence of archaeology a measure, at least, of the evidence supplied by other disciplines, in an attempt to give an overall picture of the material culture, the art and the social and economic status of our Anglo-Saxon forbears. This picture cannot be complete in a book of this length, and I can only hope that it will give a fair account, for the general reader, of the Anglo-Saxons as an organized society, seen through their material culture. The material culture of these peoples, as it survives today, is, as we shall see, of a very rich, but very limited, character. In the pagan period it is confined largely to the material found buried in graves. In the Christian period, when pagan burial practices to a large extent cease, the evidence rests largely on chance finds and such monumental remains as churches and stone crosses. Based on such sources, the picture I have painted is bound to be incomplete and in part blurred, but it represents to the best of my ability the present state of our archaeological knowledge of the Anglo-Saxon period.

CHAPTER ONE

Historical Background and Pagan Burials

To MANY the Anglo-Saxon period is seen as a no-man's-land, across which flit insubstantial, semi-legendary figures – Hengist and Horsa, Arthur, Alfred and Offa. The bleak outlines of the history of the period must be defined if we are to understand its archaeology.

It would be idle to expect to achieve a well-balanced view of Anglo-Saxon history in the course of the next few pages. Indeed, to the professional historian, the summary that follows may seem to contain merely a crude and uncritical appraisal of the period. This summary is, however, intended for the non-specialist and not for the professional historian; the opinions it contains are based on those of the leading historians of the Anglo-Saxon period, to whose works the reader is referred in the bibliography.

The history of Anglo-Saxon England must be considered in three stages: (a) the pagan period from the settlement to the Augustinian mission, (b) the establishment of England, and (c) the Scandinavian era.

THE PAGAN ANGLO-SAXON PERIOD

No period of British history is so nebulous as the fifth century. Roman government, which had collapsed as the end result of a process of decline in the first few years of the fifth century, bequeathed a legacy of Roman institutions to Britain. The Romanized native population struggled for a short time to preserve its individuality and to retain its civilization, but was gradually submerged by inroads of invaders from the Continent. 'The newcomers,' wrote the Venerable Bede,

... came from three very powerful nations of the Germans, namely the Saxons, the Angles and the Jutes. From the stock of the Jutes are the people of Kent and the people of Wight, that is, the race which holds the Isle of Wight, and that which in the province of the West Saxons is to this day called the nation of the Jutes, situated opposite that same Isle of Wight. From the Saxons, that is, from the region that now is called that of the Old Saxons, came the East Saxons, the South Saxons and the West Saxons. Further, from the Angles, that is, from the country which is called *Angulus*, and which from that time until today is said to have remained deserted between the provinces of the Jutes and Saxons, are sprung the East Angles, the Middle Angles, the Mercians, the whole race of the Northumbrians, that is, of those people who dwell north of the River Humber, and the other peoples of the Angles. ... In a short time, as bands of the aforesaid nations eagerly flocked into the island, the people of the newcomers began to increase so much that they became a source of terror to the very natives who had invited them.

This passage, written nearly three hundred years after the events it describes, is unfortunately our best historical source for the origin of the English peoples. The accuracy and exact meaning of Bede's summary of the invasions has been argued *ad nauseam*. Ultimately our best course would seem to be to take it at its face value: the account is presumably based on legend and oral tradition, but Bede – a most careful and exact scholar – has apparently simplified a very complicated story.

First of all he mentions that the 'newcomers' – the Anglo-Saxons as we more conveniently call them – were *invited* to come to England by the native inhabitants. These invited peoples were *laeti*, mercenary soldiers brought to Britain towards the end of the Roman period to help defend the country against attack from Ireland, Scotland and the Continent; traces of their pottery, similar in form to that of their homeland, have been identified at a number of Roman military sites (Caister-on-Sea, Caister-by-Norwich, York, etc.) and at one very important civil site (Mucking, Essex). Secondly, Bede specifies the homelands of these people [Fig. 2]. The Saxons came from North Germany and Holland, from the area which was known in his day as Old

Saxony, the Angles from the south of the Danish peninsula, from the area which is still called Angeln, and the Jutes from Jutland. In other words, the Anglo-Saxons came from the western coastlands of Europe, from the area between the mouth of the Rhine and central Jutland. Their invasions must be seen against the background of similar tribal movements throughout Europe, movements which are so important that the contemporary period on the Continent is designated 'the Migration period'.

A sixth-century Byzantine writer, Procopius, divides the invaders of Britain into two, Angles and Frisians, and there is probably a kernel of truth in his statement. Although the Frisians apparently inhabited the coastland of North Holland, it is possible that at this time the Frisians and Saxons had merged into one people, the Frisians losing their identity in the process, a not uncommon occurrence in the Migration period. In fact, by the time the English settlement had got under way it is probable that all these peoples, Angles, Saxons and Frisians, and to a lesser extent the more independent Jutes, had become more or less identified with each other, an opinion which is to a certain extent supported by the mixed character and origin of the earliest Anglo-Saxon grave-goods. The Anglo-Saxon peoples, then, were probably of mixed stock, with a number of common characteristics, before they arrived in England.

The invaders came in bands, headed by aristocratic leaders, to settle in a new land, at first in small groups, later combining into larger units. The date of the most important incursions of the Anglo-Saxons took place, Myres has argued, 'within ten years of the middle of the fifth century'. Our knowledge of the course of the invasions is based on both archaeological and historical sources – neither of them very secure. They came both in the guise of colonists and as mercenaries.

That the Roman policy of employing mercenaries was continued in the post-Roman period is well illustrated by the history of the semi-legendary Vortigern and Hengist and Horsa. Vortigern, 'a proud tyrant', employed Teutonic mercenaries under two leaders, Hengist and Horsa, to help him repel the Picts and the Scots. The colony, founded by Vortigern in the east of England, must have been strengthened by accretion from the Conti-

Fig. 2. Kingdoms and peoples of Anglo-Saxon England. Inset: the Continental homeland of the Anglo-Saxons. (Scale approx. ½ main map)

nent, until the mercenaries rebelled against their employers and started to colonize the country in earnest. The names of these people may be legendary but it is reasonable to suppose that parts of England – Kent and Sussex for instance – were settled in this manner. The conquest of the rest of England probably started, as did the colonization of America, with small bands camping on the eastern seaboard and gradually spreading west up the river valleys into the rest of the country. The Britons, under such legendary heroes as Arthur, for example, put up a considerable resistance against the Saxons. Gradually, however, over a period of some hundred and fifty years they were reduced to the position of a subject population, or fled to the hills and fastnesses of the Celtic lands to the west and north. At the time of the Augustinian mission the Anglo-Saxons controlled the whole of England from Kent to East Dorset and from the East Coast to the lower Severn, Staffordshire and Derbyshire, most of Yorkshire and part of Northumberland and Durham. The conquest of Britain continued sporadically for many years – the Edwardian wars of the Middle Ages are but the logical conclusions of an expansion that was continuous from the middle of the fifth century.

THE ESTABLISHMENT OF ENGLAND

The presence of a large number of tribal leaders in the early years of the settlement resulted in the establishment in England of numerous royal dynasties. The relations between those dynasties was more often bloody than friendly, but there is good reason to believe that the new settlers regarded themselves more as Anglo-Saxons than as members of their own particular kingdom. The late sixth and seventh centuries are often lumped together by historians under the heading 'the period of the heptarchy'. There were, however, more than the seven kingdoms implied in this title existing at one period or another. These were Northumbria (occasionally divided into two kingdoms – Bernicia, between the Tees and the Forth, and Deira, between the Humber and the Tees), Lindsey (roughly Lincolnshire and East Anglia), Mercia (roughly the present-day Midlands), Essex, Middlesex, Kent,

Wessex and Sussex, which were all at one time or another kingdoms, with kings who traced their ancestry from Woden or from
another Germanic god, Seaxneat. The history of the period from
600 to the Conquest tells of the gradual movement of the main
centre of power from north to south, from Northumbria to Wessex. It is also the story of the reduction of the power of these
kingdoms and their ultimate unification under one man.

One of the most important influences of the period was, of
course, that provided by the Church. The mission of St Augustine, which started in 596, and the consequent conversion of the
country, were to bring literacy to the Anglo-Saxons and organization to the central government; but, as Sir Frank Stenton has
pointed out, the church was more a hindrance than a help to the
unity of the country. The establishment of the Archbishopric of
York, in 734, for example, split the ecclesiastical and, to some
extent, the secular government of the country into two. Northumbria was throughout the middle period of Anglo-Saxon history
regarded as a distinctly separate part of the country; as witness,
for instance, King Alfred's use of the terms 'on this side of the
Humber' and 'beyond the Humber' in the introduction to his
translation of Gregory's *Cura Pastoralis*.

In the early days of Anglo-Saxon Christianity, Northumbria
was the most important kingdom in England. In the seventh
century the Northumbrian kings, Edwin, Oswald and Oswiu,
came within an ace of establishing a permanent overlordship
over the whole of England. But in 658 this hope of unity was
ended by the revolt of the Mercians, when Wulfhere took the
throne of Mercia. Although we have a clear picture of the kings
of Northumbria from the hand of Bede, himself a Northumbrian,
the northern kingdom never again achieved the power it had
under Edwin and Oswald.

Meanwhile Mercia had absorbed the kingdoms of Essex and
East Anglia (with Lindsey), the rulers of these two areas becom-
ing subject to their Mercian overlord. By about 670, London, the
great mercantile centre of England, had come under their control. During Wulfhere's reign Wessex became subject to Mercia,
as did Sussex and the Isle of Wight. Wulfhere was defeated by
the Northumbrians at the end of his reign and his successor,

Æthelbald, was left to complete the task of building up Mercian supremacy over the whole of England. It was Æthelbald's cousin Offa (757–96) who was to be the strongest Mercian king, *rex totius Anglorum patriae* (King of the whole of England) as he described himself in one of his charters. In 796 Cenwulf succeeded Offa and until 821, when he died, Mercian supremacy remained firm and established. Over a number of years following Cenwulf's death, however, Egbert, king of Wessex, after a series of campaigns in Mercian territory received the submission of all the lands formerly ruled by Offa. From now on, the fortunes of the royal house of Wessex were to control the Anglo-Saxon kingdom.

THE SCANDINAVIAN ERA

In the last years of the eighth century the Viking raiders descended on England and Western Europe:

'In this year,' says the *Anglo-Saxon Chronicle* under the year 793, 'dire portents appeared over Northumbria and sorely frightened the people. They consisted of immense whirlwinds and flashes of lightning, and fiery dragons were seen flying in the air. A great famine immediately followed those signs, and a little after that in the same year, on 8 June, the ravages of heathen men miserably destroyed God's church on Lindisfarne, with plunder and slaughter.'

They came to a land, rich and comparatively peaceful, to plunder, pillage, rob and rape. England was a home of learning, the centre of a prosperous merchant and agricultural community, and was completely unprepared for the sudden menace from the Scandinavian lands of the misty North. At first the invaders came in small bands merely to plunder, but, by the middle of the ninth century, great organized armies were ravaging the countryside. Mercia and Northumbria were conquered by the invaders and Wessex was sore pressed. Alfred's defeat of the Viking marauders at Edington in 878 called a halt to a series of Viking victories which had brought much of England under the control of the Scandinavians. From 878 and onwards, under Alfred and his successors, the Viking raiders, who had now settled in the north and east of England, were gradually brought under the control of the English crown.

Traditionally these early Vikings are known as Danes, although doubtless by the time they were settled in England they were a people of mixed Scandinavian blood. In the early years of the tenth century Lancashire and Cheshire, and the north-west generally, were invaded from Ireland by a group of Norwegian Vikings and the internecine wars between the two elements, Danish and Norwegian, considerably aided the conquest of Northumbria by the Mercians and the West Saxons under Edward the Elder and Æthelstan, who has been described as the most brilliant of English kings. Not only did Æthelstan conquer the north and establish friendly relations with its aristocracy, but he also conquered Cornwall and became one of the elder statesmen of Europe, consulted by the Emperor, the Normans and the Scandinavians. He established a sound civil service and reformed the coinage. From the death of Æthelstan in 939 there is a marked decline in the strength and prestige of the English kings. Wars with Viking raiders and bad counsel at home depleted the strength of the kingdom and only under Edgar (959–75) was any of the former brilliance of English government achieved. Edgar's greatest achievements were in the field of artistic patronage and in the monastic revival that took place under the great churchmen Oswald, Æthelwold and Dunstan – the latter credited by one chronicler with 'holy guile'.

In the years following Edgar's death the Viking attacks were renewed and, although these were resisted with spirit and some success, the conquest of England by Sweyn and Canute in the early years of the eleventh century was a foregone conclusion. Canute came to the throne of England in 1016 and for nineteen years governed from England an Empire which, in name at least, extended from the shores of the Baltic to the Isles of Scilly. The great Anglo-Scandinavian Empire could only be controlled by an immensely strong king and collapsed in 1042 on the death of Harthacnut, the son of Canute. The English dynasty of Wessex regained the throne in the person of Edward the Confessor, who had grown up at the court of the Dukes of Normandy. During his reign Norman influence in England increased, the church, the law and the administration being influenced by contemporary French institutions. These Norman elements in pre-Conquest England were, to a certain extent, counteracted by the rude Anglo-Saxon nationalism of William's distant cousin, Harold. When, on the death of Edward and the succession of Harold, William, Duke of Normandy, claimed the English throne, England was to some extent prepared for Norman government. Much that was good in Anglo-Saxon England survived the Norman Conquest which centralized the government of the country and unified England once and for all.

PAGAN ANGLO-SAXON ARCHAEOLOGY

Even today, despite the advances in settlement excavation, the archaeology of the pagan Anglo-Saxon period can best be studied in the material deposited in graves, in the brooches, buckles, weapons and pottery. Much of this material will be treated in greater detail under separate headings in later chapters of this book. Here I wish to discuss the implications of this material in a broader context.

The Anglo-Saxon peoples practised both inhumation and cremation in the burial of their dead. The two rites take many forms and are even, occasionally, mixed – skeletons being found which have only been partly consumed by fire. Although most Anglo-Saxon inhumations were in an extended position, crouched burials, in which the body has been buried with the knees beneath the chin, are by no means unknown. Other variations also occur. At Abingdon, for example, one skeleton lay on its face with the left arm raised and bent across the forehead. Sometimes a double burial is found, where the body has been placed in an old grave with the underlying body disturbed and disarticulated; occasionally two bodies were buried side by side. Cremation can also take various forms, though usually the burnt bones were collected and placed in an urn. Both inhumation and cremation burials occur in flat cemeteries and in barrows and mounds. The occurrence of mixed inhumation/cremation cemeteries is frequently recorded, even in the West Saxon area, where the ritual was more usually inhumation – out of 201 graves excavated at Abingdon, Berks., for example, 82 were cremations. In Kent and the Saxon region cremation was practised chiefly in the earliest phases of settlement, but even in these areas late cremation graves are occasionally found. In Anglian parts of the country cremation was practised alongside inhumation at all times, although the latter is apparently commoner towards the end of the pagan period. The only cremation cemeteries without inhumations are in the Anglian region.

The Anglo-Saxons did not normally use the old Romano-British cemeteries. At Mucking, Essex, for example, the Anglo-Saxon cemetery was at some distance from its Romano-British fore-runner. But continuity can sometimes be demonstrated: the Anglo-Saxon cemetery on the Mount at York was in the middle of one of the Roman city's principal grave-fields, while at Frilford and Long Wittenham the Anglo-Saxon cemetery was related closely to an earlier Roman burial ground. Such cases are rare and may be, as Dr Myres suggests, so sited because both here and in their homeland on the Continent the Anglo-Saxons centred their grave-fields on places, such as prehistoric burial mounds, which had already been sanctified. (This practice is paralleled at a later date, when the pagan Vikings buried their dead in Christian churchyards in northern England.) Perhaps one of the main reasons for this lack of continuity in the use of cemeteries between the Roman and Anglo-Saxon periods is the fact that the Anglo-Saxons often settled in areas not intensively used by the Romano-British population.

The Anglo-Saxon dead were buried with their most intimate personal possessions – brooches, work-box and chatelaine in the case of a woman, spear, shield and sword in the case of a man. Occasionally they were buried with food (at Melbourn a sheep's jaw was found in a grave, while at another Cambridgeshire cemetery eggs were found in an urn) and drink, which was held in pottery vessels (e.g. Fig. 20c). In cremation burials personal possessions were often burnt with the body; if not, they were often represented by small, unburnt model combs, knives, etc., placed in the urn with the ashes. Features such as the food and the model tools suggest that this is something more than the habit found in a number of modern societies of dressing up a corpse in its best clothes. The body was being sent off into the after-life with the belongings it would need there, some men even being placed in their ship, as at Snape. Occasionally a slave would be sacrificed and placed in a grave, but evidence of such a practice is not commonly found. A most dramatic example of this practice was recorded at Sewerby, Yorkshire, where a woman had been flung face-down, still alive, into a half-filled grave and weighed down by a quern-stone which had been thrown on top of her.

As the surviving vernacular literature was written by Christians – usually by priests – it is hardly surprising that there is in this country little written evidence concerning pagan burial practices. We have to turn to the evidence provided by the Scandinavian literature for information concerning such burial rites. The following passage from *Ynglinga Saga* is typical of many passages which could be quoted here:

The burning was carried out in a splendid manner. At that time it was believed that the higher the smoke rose in the air, the loftier would be the position of the burnt man in heaven; and the more possessions that were buried with him the richer he would be.

The great Anglo-Saxon epic poem *Beowulf* yields some evidence regarding the practices of pagan burial. Consider, for example, the burial of Beowulf himself:

Then the people of the Geats, as he had asked them, constructed a splendid pyre on the ground, hung with helmets, war shields and shining corselets, in the midst of which the lamenting warriors laid the glorious prince, their beloved lord. Then the warriors began to light the greatest of funeral pyres on the hill, the wood smoke rose high, black above the fire; the roaring flame mingled with the weeping (the tumult of the wind ceased) until it had consumed the body hot to its heart. . . . The people of the Wedra then raised a high, broad barrow on the cliff; it could be seen from afar by seafarers; in ten days they built the beacon of the bold warrior. They surrounded the remains of the pyre with a wall, constructed as worthily as skilled men could do. They laid rings and jewels in the barrow.

The passage then tails off into semi-Christian sentiment, but the pagan elements are plain. Among other funerals recorded in Beowulf is one in which a ship is loaded with the body and treasure, and pushed out to sea.

The idea of a journey to the world of the dead is almost as universal as is the idea of furnishing the body with weapons, tools, ornaments and food. It would be tedious to labour the point. However, it is as a result of the Anglo-Saxons' belief in this idea that we have the large quantity of pagan Saxon material in our museums today.

THE ARCHAEOLOGY OF THE ANGLO-SAXON SETTLEMENT

From 1913 until his death in 1955 E. T. Leeds, in a series of books and articles, attempted, on the basis of a minute study of the archaeological material, to define the areas of the Anglian, Saxon and Jutish settlement. This was mainly based on a typological study of the humbler type of Anglo-Saxon brooch. One of his most important observations, however, is based on a geographical fact: Anglo-Saxon cemeteries, he noted, bore no distributional relationship to the Roman road system; the newcomers advanced into, and settled, the country along the river valleys. He further pointed out that the Anglo-Saxons also avoided the Roman towns and forts, the great deserted stone buildings of the Romans which were described in the literature as the 'cunning work of giants'. We have already noted that continuity in the use of cemeteries between the Roman and Anglo-Saxon periods is rare. This lack of interest on the part of the Saxons in the social machinery of Roman Britain – in its daily life, its communications, its villa system, its organized army and its central government – is an interesting and unexplained feature of their settlement. Leeds's picture of this *horror romani* needs perhaps a little qualification today. Professor Frere's recent excavations have shown that there was a Saxon settlement of an extremely early period within the Roman town at Canterbury and there were certainly two early cremation cemeteries of some size at York. Again, it is clear that in north and east Kent, at any rate, the Anglo-Saxon cemeteries are closely related in their distribution to the Roman roads.

Leeds's attempt to distinguish the Anglian, Saxon and Jutish elements in the burial material met with varying success. We have seen how the national character of the newcomers at the time of the invasions was already very mixed: this mixture is reflected in the archaeological material. Certain features of the Saxon element among the invaders, however, are clearly distinguishable. The distribution of early saucer brooches, for example, as studied by Mr Leeds and more recently by Mrs Morris, shows a concentration in south-east England and the Thames Valley – an area traditionally designated Saxon. Such saucer brooches have their origin on the lower Rhine, in the area of the Saxon homeland. Similarly a group of small cruciform brooches, of an early date, found in Kent and paralleled to some extent in the Danish material, help to vindicate Bede's statement as to the Jutish origin of the Kentish people. Dr Myres suggested that a study of the pottery would seem to indicate that East Anglia received more direct immigration from Schleswig than did Northumbria, which, as Mr Hunter Blair has pointed out, came under Anglo-Saxon rule as much as a result of the revolt of Anglo-Saxon mercenaries employed by the Romano-Britons as by direct colonization. But generally speaking the archaeological material of the period of settlement is so mixed that attempts to distinguish it tribally are vain.

There is a good deal of archaeological evidence to show that there were Anglo-Saxon mercenaries in Britain before the Roman abandonment of the province. The mercenaries took over the districts which were too weak to oppose them and invited their cousins from across the North Sea to come and share their spoils. The mercenaries were presumably of very mixed origin, as were their cousins, and they combined to contribute to the muddle that comprises the archaeological record, a muddle in which, in a single cemetery, older Roman-Saxon pottery occurs alongside both Anglian and Saxon pottery and in which Saxon brooches occur in both Anglian, Saxon and Jutish areas.

Broadly speaking, however, once the preliminary muddle of the invasion period was over, and once the newcomers had become established, certain features in the archaeological material clearly distinguish the Essex–Wessex–Sussex area from the Yorkshire–Mercia–Suffolk area and both of these from the rich Kentish area. How much of this material is tribal in the sense of 'Anglian', 'Saxon' or 'Jutish', and how much is regional, is a problem that must now be examined.

One of the chief archaeological features of Anglo-Saxon Kent is the garnet-ornamented jewellery – for although some of this jewellery occurs elsewhere, it has long been obvious that it is mainly concentrated within that county. The discovery, however, of a large quantity of garnet jewellery at Sutton Hoo in Suffolk encourages the archaeologist to reconsider his previously held views. For the Sutton Hoo jewellery, while related in certain technical features to the Kentish material, has also many unique features. The differences are sufficient to enable us to recognize a distant Kentish culture, at once individual and wealthy, which must be based almost completely on economic circumstance and not on tribal differences. Kent's geographical position and its rich soils have always made it a wealthy county. Most scholars nowadays would agree that this garnet jewellery flourished in the last half of the sixth century and in the first half of the seventh, and that it reflects the richness and importance of the settled area, an importance which can be seen, for example, in the historical figure of King Æthelbert of Kent who had strong Continental connexions. But to call this jewellery 'Jutish', as is so often done, is to miss the whole significance of the Kentish problem. Dr Hodgkin clarified the position when he said, 'The Jutish nation ... was made after the Conquest. It was to all intents made in Kent.' In fact some historians have been using the word 'Jutish' when they meant 'Kentish'. Bede's *Jutarum natio* in Kent and the Isle of Wight has been torn from its context; it means surely that the earliest settlers in those areas were organized under leaders from Jutland and received reinforcements from that area as well as from other Northern European areas. It follows that once the newcomers had become established in the Kentish area they would, under the influence of their new environment and of their geographical situation in relation to the Franks, develop a material culture of their own, just as they developed a legal system and a nation of their own.

Our picture of the material culture of the Angles and the Saxons is not quite so well defined. The archaeological evidence within the areas occupied by these peoples rests largely on a study of their jewellery, the Anglo-Saxon equivalent of the mass-produced jewellery sold today in the cheaper chain stores. The distribution of this material, when divided typologically, falls into two groups which can be classed as Anglian and Saxon. For instance, as we have seen, one of the leading Saxon types of brooch is the saucer brooch, which has a distributional concentration in the Upper Thames Valley, Sussex and Berkshire, with a number of outliers in the southern Midlands. This type of brooch is reasonably common in the continental Saxon homeland and its Saxon distribution in England is quite convincing. Similarly the small group of wrist clasps appear to be typically Anglian, if judged only by their geographical distribution. I believe, however, that we must be rather more careful in attaching these tribal names to objects just because they are found in the broad area in question. The distribution of a certain type of cruciform brooch (Åberg III and IV) is clearly centred on the Cambridge region, with outliers in Yorkshire and Mercia. So far, admittedly, not a single brooch of this sort has been found in the Saxon region, yet the type can hardly be considered as typical of the whole Anglian area. Rather, it is a fashion that grew up in a smallish area and was then traded out of that area into other districts. Other so-called Anglian types occur over such a wide area that although they were presumably made in one particular district, is is impossible to distinguish them by any other title than 'Anglian'.

The wide distribution of objects resulting from trade must always be borne in mind. We shall revert to this subject in a later chapter, but a few examples may be quoted here to demonstrate the mobility of objects at this early stage of Anglo-Saxon history. Anglo-Saxon jewellery has been found in Germany, pottery from the Low Countries carried wine to Kent, and chatelaine rings of African ivory are of reasonably common occurrence in Anglo-Saxon graves, while cowrie shells came from the tropical waters of the Indian Ocean. When we know that objects such as these travelled thousands of miles to local markets we cannot rely too closely on a scattered distribution of a handful of cheap brooches over the whole face of England.

SUTTON HOO

Space prohibits a full discussion of the thousands of Anglo-Saxon graves found in England, but one of these graves, found at Sutton Hoo near Woodbridge in Suffolk, deserves consideration at some length. The grave produced the richest and most brilliant treasure ever found on British soil; it is, indeed, only paralleled in Europe by the funerary treasure of Childeric, King of the Franks, who died in 481. Childeric's treasure was found at Tournai in Belgium in 1653, but only a few fragments survived the robbery at the Cabinet des Medailles in Paris in 1831. Many rich graves had been found in England before the discovery of Sutton Hoo – Taplow in Buckinghamshire, Broomfield in Essex, Cowlow in Derbyshire and a whole host of graves in Kent – but all pale into insignificance by the side of this East Anglian king's treasure.

The excavators of Sutton Hoo in 1939 came to an oval mound with a central hollow, lying in a barrow cemetery on the edge of an escarpment overlooking the river Deben. The shape of the mound was eventually explained by the fact that a ship had been buried in it; the hollow in the middle proved to have been caused partly by the collapse of a wooden mortuary chamber amidships and partly by the attentions of some sixteenth- or seventeenth-century antiquarians, who had tried to rob the grave by sinking a shaft in the centre of the mound. All that remained of the ship were the marks in the sand of the decayed wood, marks which were skilfully isolated by the excavators so that a plan of the ship and photographs of it in its entirety could be made [Fig. 17]. The original overall length of the ship must have been about 29 m. It was a clinker-built ship of a type paralleled by the ship found at Nydam in South Jutland. Unlike the well-known

Viking ships, it was a rowing-boat; there was no seating for a
mast and traces of a rowlock survived on the port gunwale. No
seats or decking were found but in the centre were traces of the
gabled mortuary chamber which contained the burial deposit.

No body was found in the ship – no traces of human bones.
The burial must, then, be considered as a cenotaph, a monument
to a great man: the treasure and paraphernalia found in the
grave leave no doubt that this was the memorial of a king.

The objects found in the burial chamber can be divided into
three groups: (a) domestic utensils and minor weapons, (b) personal ornaments and personal weapons, and (c) royal regalia.
The objects classed under the first heading include a quantity of
chainwork, iron-bound wooden buckets, cauldrons, a pottery
bottle (which in form resembles the wheel-turned pottery of
Kent), a group of spears and angons (see below, p. 124), an
iron-hafted battle-axe and a number of iron objects of indeter-
minate use. The remains of a musical instrument, originally
reconstructed as a rectangular harp, but now seen to be a round
lyre, was taken to pieces before burial and placed inside a cast
bronze bowl, which had been imported from Alexandria. Also
found were the remains of two silver-mounted drinking-horns,
a number of cups with mounted rims and gourds. One of the
horns has been reconstructed and found to have a capacity of
some six quarts and must have come from the head of the now
extinct aurochs. All these objects are paralleled in other Anglo-
Saxon contexts, with the exception of the iron-hafted axe. Other
objects, however, must be classed in this group, some of which
are rather more exotic – the great circular silver dish of Byzantine origin which bears the control stamps of the Emperor
Anastasius (491–518), for example. Other pieces of Mediterranean
silver plate include a large fluted silver bowl, which was found
underneath the large dish; it bears in a central, circular field a
late classical female head in low relief. A silver ladle and a small
cup were found, together with a set of ten hemispherical silver
bowls. [Pl. 3]. In the centre of each bowl was inscribed a simple
geometrical or semi-floral design. Two very significant pieces are
a pair of spoons of a well-known classical type, which bear the
names of Saul and Paul in Greek characters. This allusion to the

conversion of the Apostle must symbolize the conversion or the baptism of an important person.

Finally, we must class in this group a series of three bronze bowls fitted with loops for suspension and ornamented with circular, and, in one case, with square as well as circular, panels of enamelled ornament. These belong to a large and common group of antiquities, known as 'hanging-bowls', which continued to be made until well on into the eighth century, some late variants being found in Viking Age graves in Scandinavia. The decoration of the applied enamelled mounts is Celtic rather than Anglo-Saxon in origin; it is most commonly based on developed spiral motifs, sometimes, as at Sutton Hoo, being further decorated with small pieces of millefiori glass floated into the enamel. These millefiori fragments are cut from a rod – of which examples have been found at Garannes in Ireland and at Bede's monastery of Jarrow – made up of many strands of different coloured glass, stretched and twisted in the fashion of the multi-coloured 'rock' popularly sold at seaside resorts. There has been a considerable amount of discussion concerning the purpose and origin of these bowls. The presence of a model fish [Pl. 11], standing on a column in the centre of the Sutton Hoo bowl, and the fact that many of the bowls have an escutcheon on the inside, suggest that they held some clear liquid; the suggestion has recently been made that they were used as a kind of ecclesiastical 'finger-bowl', although there is still a certain amount of support for the theory that they were used as sanctuary lamps. The fish in the Sutton Hoo hanging-bowl may be the well-known Christian symbol; if so, a liturgical use is not ruled out. On the other hand, if the bowl held water, the fish would then be in its natural element and its use here might merely be the craftsman's conceit. These bowls were apparently made in a Celtic area, presumably some were made in Northumbria : Dr Françoise Henry's contention that they were made exclusively in Ireland is not convincing in the face of their rarity in that country and their ubiquity in the Anglo-Saxon area.

The second group of objects in the Sutton Hoo cenotaph comprises the personal equipment which was laid out along the line of the keel, in the centre of the mortuary chamber. It forms by

far the most exciting group of objects in the grave. The three
major weapons, the sword with its jewelled pommel and scabbard
[Pl. 2], the shield with its bird and dragon figures, and the
helmet [Pl. 8], covered with plates of impressed ornament, are
closely paralleled in the rich graves of Uppland in Sweden,
whence they were almost certainly imported. All the personal
ornaments, however, are certainly of English manufacture and
are remarkable as much for their richness as their quantity. Other
than the mounts of the sword, nineteen pieces of gold jewellery
were found in the grave, the largest and most impressive of
which is the great gold buckle [Pl. 7], which is 13.2 cm. long and
weighs over fourteen ounces. The front face of the object is
covered with most skilfully interlaced, asymmetrical snakes,
bordered by interlaced, elongated animals. The loop of the buckle
has a slightly more regular, plain ribbon interlace, but the circular plate, behind the tongue, has more interlaced snakes. All
the ribbon-like bands on the buckle plate and on the circular
tongue plate are decorated with incised circles within bordering
lines, all inlaid with niello. Three great plain dome-headed rivets
connect with sliding catches on the hinged back plate.

There is a striking difference between the great gold buckle
and the more flamboyant, polychrome jewellery which makes up
the greater part of the personal ornaments. The purse-lid [Pl. 9],
for example, consisted of a border, made up of twisted wire
filigree, and panels inlaid with garnet and coloured glass which
enclosed a piece of ivory, leather or other material, in which
were set seven plaques and four studs. The plaques and studs
are inlaid with garnets and mosaic glass: in the top centre is a
plaque containing four animals, set in pairs, whose limbs interlace; this is flanked by two hexagonal mosaic plaques. Below
each of these is a plaque portraying a man between two rampant
beasts, while in the centre bottom of the purse are two affronted
plaques showing small, duck-like birds caught in the claws of
birds of prey. The height of perfection in this polychrome technique is reached in the pair of curved clasps that hinge centrally
on a gold, animal-headed pin [Pl. 1]. The clasps were sewn to
their cloth or leather base through a series of strong lugs. Each
half of the clasp is, in all major respects, similar to the others,

although there are slight variations in each piece. The curved end takes the form of two boars [Fig. 3], so interlocked that their hindquarters form the outer element of the ornament, their heads appearing in the centre. In the spaces between the heads and feet are panels of delicate filigree animal ornament. The rest of the plaque consists of a rectangular frame, ornamented

Fig. 3. Interlocked boars from the Sutton Hoo clasps

with a series of interlaced, ribbon-like creatures, which encloses a carpet pattern of polychrome cell-work. In no other piece of jewellery from Sutton Hoo does the quality of workmanship surpass that demonstrated by the clasps. The garnets are cut accurately to the shape of the cell which they fill, whether the edge be straight, curved or step-shaped. Beneath each garnet can be seen the piece of gold foil with its chequer-board pattern which reflects light back through the garnet at different angles. In this piece can be seen all the competent assurance of a first-rate craftsman. These objects, together with the many minor pieces of garnet jewellery found in the grave, form the nucleus of a corpus of jewellery which has a local East Anglian character [Pls. 4–6]. Although related in a superficial manner to the garnet jewellery of Kent, the Sutton Hoo jewellery together with a number of other pieces in the grave was apparently made in a single East Anglian workshop under a number of influences, English, Frankish and Swedish.

The third group of objects comprises the symbols of royalty, an iron standard and whetstone, which may be considered as a sceptre. The standard is made of iron, is about 188 cm. high, and consists of a long iron bar surmounted by a ring topped by a bronze-covered iron stag. At its foot is a barbed spike. Immediately below the ring are four short arms, each terminating in formalized bulls' heads. About 30 cm. below the ring is an iron grill with horned projections at the corners linked with iron bars to a point about halfway down the standard. At first it was thought that the object was a flambeau, or lampstand, but it seems more reasonable to suppose that it is in fact a standard (of the type known as *Tufa*) which Bede says was carried in front of King Edwin of Northumbria: the object is more or less unparalleled in the Europe of that time.

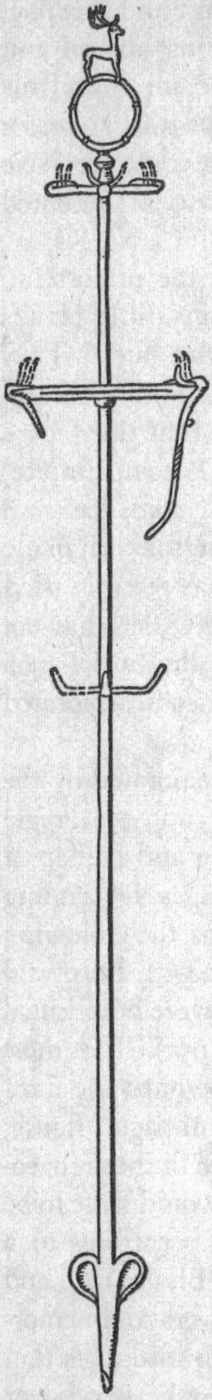

The whetstone [Pl. 10] found at Sutton Hoo shows no traces of use for any normal sharpening process; indeed the delicate carving and bronze casing at the terminals make it unlikely that it was ever intended to be used for such a purpose. Of square section, it is about 61 cm. long and tapers towards the terminals. The looped terminals are painted red and enclosed in a bronze cage. Below the terminals, at each end and on each face, is a series of human masks carved in low relief. The whole stone is ground to a finely polished surface. This object is unparalleled in the Anglo-Saxon world, although a fragment of a large whetstone decorated with crude representations of the human face has been found at Hough-on-the-Hill in Lincolnshire, and two smaller whetstones carved with human masks have been found in the Celtic west. The fact that this whetstone has no conceivable use endows it with a significance of its own. The idea that it is a sceptre has received general acceptance: in the words of Sir Thomas Kendrick, 'Nothing like this monstrous stone

Fig. 4. The standard from Sutton Hoo

exists anywhere else. It is a unique, savage thing; and inexplicable, except perhaps as a symbol proper to the king himself and the divinity and mystery which surrounded the smith and his tools in the northern world.' Whether we accept it as a sceptre or as a wand of office and authority is immaterial; we have something here that is outside the run of material normally found in Anglo-Saxon graves.

Lastly, mention must be made of objects of the utmost importance – the coins. There were thirty-seven coins, three blanks and two small ingots, all of gold, in the Sutton Hoo burial. They were originally enclosed in the purse, of which only the lid mounts survive. The coins were all *tremises* (one-third of a solidus, the standard imperial gold coin of the Roman Empire) and were all struck in France. The dating of the coins has been the subject of considerable discussion. Dr Grierson originally dated their deposition to 650–60, but Dr Kent has recently tried to re-date them to 625–30. Unfortunately the new date has not been universally accepted and attempts to fix the burial in a chronological context and to identify the person commemorated by this cenotaph remain controversial.

There can be little doubt that the man commemorated by the deposition of such elaborate grave-goods and apparent regal symbols was a royal personage – probably a king and perhaps a member of the East Anglian dynasty, the Wuffingas. Depending on the date of deposition indicated by the coins the following kings could be commemorated: Redwald (d. 624–5), Eorpwald (d. 627/8 or 632/3), Sigebehrt and Ecgric (who were both killed in 640/1), Anna (d. 654) and Æthelhere (d. 655). The most attractive candidate is undoubtedly Redwald, perhaps the most important member of the family and a rich semi-pagan figure, but in my view the date of his death is too early to fit the archaeological evidence, even the numismatic evidence would have to be stretched to fill the gap. Anna was buried – according to a reasonably reliable source – in the monastery at Blythburgh and this could be his cenotaph only if his pagan followers commemorated their master in this traditional fashion as an insurance that his soul should be well provided for after death, whichever religion proved efficacious. It seems unlikely that Sigebehrt would be commemorated in such a fashion by the strongly Christian Anna, for Sigebehrt had been a monk until forced out of a monastery to take part in Ecgric's campaign against an invasion of East Anglia by Penda of Mercia. Ecgric and Æthelhere both died heros' deaths in battle and it could be reasonably argued that they best fulfilled the requirements of the age when a man's greatest achievement could be death with his troops. Eorpwald, Ecgric or Æthelhere, any of these could be commemorated by this cenotaph. We may never identify him but the unknown king has left his memorial and we can only admire the riches and glories of the East Anglian royal family who numbered among their treasures the finest jewellery produced in Europe at that time, as well as riches imported from the exotic Mediterranean world. The king who was commemorated by this burial must be seen as the peer of any Germanic or Saxon king in Western Europe.

CHAPTER TWO

Christian Antiquities

596: In this year Pope Gregory sent Augustine to England with a good number of monks, who preached God's word to the English people.

THUS, laconically, does the *Anglo-Saxon Chronicle* dismiss the Christian mission to England. The conversion of England was a long process; it was many decades, for example, before pagan burial practices ceased completely. Gradually, however, grave-goods become of less importance in contributing to our knowledge of the Anglo-Saxons and a different class of antiquity takes their place. Churches, chalices, crosses and manuscripts replace the pots and brooches, the swords and the jewellery of the illiterate pagan population. The church brought with it Mediterranean learning and ideas; it brought writing and architecture, sculpture and painting to add colour and sophistication to the life of the English.

Christianity was not unknown in Britain before the advent of St Augustine; in the north and west there was an active Celtic church, founded while the Romans still ruled the country. Missionaries of this church travelled from Scotland and Ireland to the Continent, apparently leaving the Saxon invader to his own gods and his own beliefs. In Kent, King Aethelbert had married a Christian princess, Bertha, the daughter of the Frankish king Charibert, and she had brought with her a Frankish bishop named Liuthard. But it was Augustine who was to convert Æthelbert and Kent. The slow and tedious business of the conversion of England then began in earnest and perhaps the greatest triumph of the mission was the conversion of King Edwin of Northumbria in 626. For the missionaries, however, it was uphill work and there were many setbacks before England was finally converted.

We have few, if any, relics of pre-Augustinian Christianity in Anglo-Saxon England. There are a number of churches of Roman date in this country but very few churches, or fragments of churches, now survive which were used in the period between the departure of the Romans and the Augustinian mission, and the evidence for their use is slender. One such is the church of St Martin at Canterbury where a portion of the chancel may be part of the ancient church which Queen Bertha had used before the arrival of St Augustine. Sir Eric Fletcher has recently suggested that the church at Stone, Kent, may perhaps have been part of a pre-Augustinian church.

One of the principal sites of the conversion has been revealed by excavations at Yeavering, Northumberland. Yeavering was the site of one of the palaces of Paulinus's royal convert, the Northumbrian king Edwin. The preliminary report draws attention to the most remarkable feature found on the site, namely traces of a large timber grand-stand resembling in plan the triangular *cuneus* of a Roman theatre. This was almost certainly the meeting place, or moot, of the local assembly and it is tempting to imagine Paulinus preaching from the platform at the focus of the structure. We must await Dr Hope-Taylor's final report on his excavations, but buildings were certainly found on the site which may be interpreted as churches, while one of them was possibly a pagan temple which had been converted to Christian use.

The basic church of the Anglo-Saxon period consisted of a nave and a chancel covered with a pitched roof or roofs. In the chancel was the altar. Various ancillary elements were added to this basic pattern – porches, porticuses, crypts, towers, western galleries and even, in the latest period, transepts. Churches were built of wood, stone, brick, or a mixture of either two or three of these. Although from literary sources we know of timber churches at Lindisfarne, Glastonbury and Chester-le-Street, only a single wooden church of the Anglo-Saxon period survives – the rather mutilated church of Greensted in the wooded county of Essex. This is a 'stave-church', built of vertical timbers in the

Scandinavian fashion and probably erected early in the eleventh century when Danish kings ruled England.

Recent work by Dr and Mrs Taylor suggests that more than three hundred Anglo-Saxon churches or fragments of churches survive and, although some of these may be strictly speaking of post-Conquest date, this enables us to characterize their main features in order to define the architecture of the period. Although there is a large quantity of Anglo-Saxon ecclesiastical architecture, it is scattered throughout the country in areas where different building materials are used and chronologically it spans more than four hundred years and buildings of varying functions, importance and richness. One must, therefore, generalize with caution. A number of surviving churches or fragments of churches can be dated on firm grounds. We know, for example, that the church of St Peter and Paul at Canterbury was built in the lifetime of St Augustine and that part of the surviving church

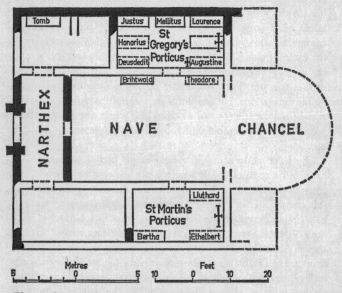

Fig. 5. Ground-plan of church of SS. Peter and Paul, Canterbury (after Clapham)

at Monkwearmouth was consecrated in 674, and it is possible that certain surviving fragments of the sister church at Jarrow were consecrated in 684 (the dedication stone survives). A few other churches can be dated, but most of them are of tenth- or eleventh-century date. Other churches and architectural fragments can only be dated on the basis of individual architectural features which have been defined as specifically Anglo-Saxon.

What then are the main features of Anglo-Saxon architecture? Firstly, the ground-plan is of little significance in recognizing an Anglo-Saxon church. Most surviving churches consist simply of a rectangular nave and a rectangular chancel. Some early Kentish churches have a curved east end and in the same area churches are found with chambers (porticuses) leading off the nave, while some very late churches have transepts. (A distinctive feature is the occasional presence of a number of churches close together on the same axis, best seen at the monastery of St Augustine in Canterbury where four separate churches are set in line.) Further it is impossible to date any piece of walling on the basis of technique alone; the Anglo-Saxon mason used any available stone from dressed flint to ashlar and only by examining the quoins and secondary detail is it possible to recognize – in some cases at least – a pre-Conquest structure. The most distinctive form of Anglo-Saxon quoining is long-and-short work, in which long upright dressed stones of regular size alternate with a long horizontal dressed stone at the corner of a building, as at Earl's Barton [Pl. 12]. A related form of quoining is 'megalithic side-alternating quoining', in which large dressed blocks, higher than the normal masonry coursing, are set alternately with their narrow ends on different faces of the wall. Similarly the use of really large stone quoins may be indicative of an Anglo-Saxon building, but many buildings have no such feature. The walls were often plastered both internally and externally and were often, in the later period especially, panelled with strip work of rectangular cross-section. This can be seen at Earl's Barton [Pl. 12] and Bradford-on-Avon [Pl. 15], at both of which the panelling is very elaborate. In some cases string courses and other similar architectural details are ornamented, or carved panels are inserted in a wall either singly or as part of a decorative scheme –

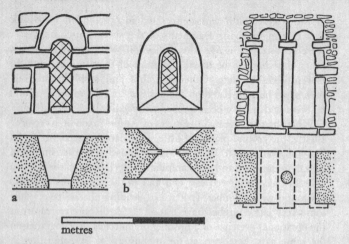

metres

Fig. 6. Architectural details from Anglo-Saxon churches: (a) window with single-splayed opening; (b) window with double-splayed opening; (c) belfry opening, showing mid-wall shaft and through stones

the most elaborate example of this can be seen at Breedon-on-the-Hill, Leicestershire, where the sculptures have survived the church. As with most medieval architecture the wall openings – arches, doors, windows – are most distinctive of the period. Apart from a few triangular-headed doors and windows [Pl. 12], mostly probably late, all Anglo-Saxon arches have round heads. The heads are either carved out of a single stone or consist of irregular voussoirs with no distinctive keystone [Pl. 13]. Windows [Fig. 6] tend to have a single internal splay, but are splayed internally and externally in the later period (at Bradford-on-Avon, Pl. 15, some single splayed windows have been re-cut in the latest fashion). Later in the period belfry openings [Fig. 6c] often consist of a double opening with a mid-wall shaft supporting a slab of the thickness of the wall. Windows were sometimes glazed. It is recorded, for instance, that Benedict Biscop imported glaziers from Gaul in the seventh century and remains of their handiwork have been found during excavations of the monasteries at Monkwearmouth and Jarrow. The glass was made in a number of colours from deep red to white and was set in lead channels to give a mosaic-like effect.

The greater arches are generally rather narrow and of a single order, but sometimes they have a hood moulding (a piece of strip work concentric with the circumference of the arch). In many cases the jambs of the arch are lined with large stones which go through the thickness of the wall set alternately horizontal and upright in the manner seen in the chancel at Escomb, County Durham [Pl. 13], which gave its name to the technique, 'Escomb fashion' (the same feature also occurs in minor openings). Like those of the windows, the voussoirs are irregular and there is no deliberately formed keystone. The imposts are usually square but are sometimes constructed of a series of over-sailing slabs and sometimes (as at Escomb, Pl. 13) chamfered.

Among architectural details which are used in a number of situations one of the most striking is the baluster shaft. In early contexts, as in the seventh-century church at Monkwearmouth, they are of cylindrical form; while in later examples – in the belfry openings at Earl's Barton [Pl. 12], for example – the shafts have a marked central swelling.

In this summary description of Anglo-Saxon ecclesiastical architecture there have been many generalizations. But the architectural features described here can be used as a rough scale to set against surviving stone buildings of the Anglo-Saxon period, be they great monasteries like Christ Church at Canterbury, minsters like that at Winchester (which is now being revealed by excavation), great semi-military structures like Earl's Barton, small churches like Escomb, or simple cells of which only casual traces remain.

Benedict Biscop imported not only glaziers, but also masons. The pagan Anglo-Saxons had built in wood and regarded the stone building of the Romans with awe as the 'cunning work of giants'. It is significant that the Christian church, with its Mediterranean background, re-introduced the art of the mason into this country and with it the art of the stone carver. There must be nearly 2,500 known fragments of Anglo-Saxon sculpture in England and South Scotland, and, although many of them are decorative architectural features, a good many of them take the

form of crosses and tombstones. The large stone crosses, sometimes 5 m. high, which occur especially in the north of England,
must be taken as marking preaching places or meeting places.
It has been suggested that, when a community could not afford
to build a church, a cross of wood or stone was erected and made
the centre for Christian worship. There is a certain amount of
evidence for this argument, despite the fact that many crosses
are so rich that a small wooden church could have been built for
the same price and in the same time as it would take to raise a
cross. From the literature we learn that Willibald, who later
became the missionary bishop of Eichstätt, was taken as a sick
child 'to the cross of the Saviour, it being the custom of the
Saxon people to erect a cross for the daily service of prayer on
the estates of good and noble men, where there was no church'.
The surviving crosses nearly all stood in a churchyard, and
such of them as do occur in the market-place of a town, as at
Sandbach in Cheshire, were presumably removed there at the
period of the Reformation. Even when there was a church they
would be used as a centre for preaching. St Oswald of Worcester,
for example, in the tenth century, frequently preached near a
memorial cross to congregations that were too big for his church.
Such crosses as that from Bewcastle in Cumberland, or Ruthwell
in Dumfriesshire [Pl. 53], form part of a large group which
occurred, to use Sir Thomas Kendrick's words, 'as a comprehen-
sible advertisement for the Bible story'. It is conceivable that in
some cases the crosses were erected to replace a wooden cross
put up by the original missionary of the area, as a commemora-
tion of the conversion, but such theories are incapable of proof.
Many of these crosses were overthrown during the Reformation;
an Act of the Assembly of the Church of Scotland, for instance,
dated 1642, ordered the 'idolatrous monuments at Ruthwall' to
be demolished.

Memorial crosses and tombstones vary considerably in size
and shape. Some memorial stones, such as the so-called pillow
stones from Hartlepool, were actually buried in the grave; they
are square and bear a cross with the name of the person commemorated engraved on the surface. Others, the tenth-century
hog's-backed tombstones of the north-west of England for ex-

ample, are recumbent stones with the shape of a pitched roof. The vast majority took the form of crosses, as much as 3 m. high, erected as headstones to graves. The tombstones are immediately derived from Roman prototypes, which are quite common in this country, and from the Celtic tombstones so often encountered in western Britain; they are certainly not a characteristic of the pagan Germanic forbears of the Anglo-Saxons.

From literary sources we learn of the richness of church treasuries of the Anglo-Saxon period. Between 970 and the Norman Conquest the Abbey of Ely, for example, received many gifts, including four silver-gilt figures of virgin saints, set with precious stones, a gold crucifix, many silver and gold crosses, one at least bearing a figure of Christ, a shrine decorated with gold and precious stones to hold the relics of St Wendreda, a life-size seated figure of the Virgin and Child in gold and silver, an episcopal cross, a silver ciborium in the shape of a tower, chalices, patens, censers and a large quantity of rich textiles. Many of these objects disappeared when the monks of Ely paid William the Conqueror a fine in 1074: on this occasion the figures of the four virgins, the figures of the Virgin and Child, crosses, altars, shrines, book-covers, chalices, patens, bowls, buckets, chalice-pipes, cups and dishes were sacrificed to raise the required one thousand marks. Such objects rarely survive: but two great finds allow a glimpse of the trappings of the Christian Church. The first is the Coffin of St Cuthbert, and the second the Trewhiddle Hoard.

On 17 May 1827 a party of clerics and workmen gathered in the feretory of Durham Cathedral to open the reputed grave of St Cuthbert, who had died in 687 at his hermitage on Farne Island. The shrine of the saint had been pillaged at the Reformation and a very circumstantial account survives of the breaking-open of the coffin and its reburial by Henry VIII's Commissioners. Happily the body of the saint, with the light wooden coffin dating from the seventh century, survived with some of the other contents of the coffin until the nineteenth-century opening of the tomb. The members of the Cathedral chapter, when they opened the tomb, found not only the skeleton of St Cuthbert and relics of other saints, but certain objects placed in the tomb either at the time of his original burial or at one of the many later re-openings of the tomb during the early Middle Ages. Only five objects of a date roughly contemporary with St Cuthbert survive: these are the pectoral cross of the Saint, the portable altar, the comb, a gospel book and the coffin itself.

The pectoral cross [Pl. 40], which has a span of 6 cm., is of gold inset with garnets in a cell pattern made up of adjacent rectangles, with a circular garnet at the centre and a loop for suspension. It is hollow, built on a base-plate; a cylindrical collar in the centre carries the circular garnet which rests on a white shell imported from tropical waters. The garnets in the centre and those on the arms are bordered by billeted and beaded edgings and by dummy rivets in the shape of small cylinders of gold crowned by a golden granule. The cross is remarkable in that it is a Christian object carried out in the technique of the pagan Anglo-Saxon jeweller. Other crosses in this technique are known from Wilton and Ixworth [Pls. 41, 42], and a small pendant gold cross with a central garnet occurs in the Desborough necklace. Taken together, these objects show that there was no immediate change in the fashions of jewellery with the introduction of Christianity, for they closely resemble the garnet jewellery of the pagan period; but we shall discuss this matter below.

The portable altar of St Cuthbert is the earliest but not the only, portable altar of the Anglo-Saxon period. Originally it was a small block of oak forming a rectangle measuring 13.3 by 12 cm., inscribed IN HONOREM S PETRU ('in honour of St Peter') and carved with five crosses, one in the centre and one in each corner. Either during the Saint's lifetime or within a few years of his death a silver shrine was added to the altar, enclosing it completely. The silver plates are decorated in an embossed technique. On one side is a now fragmentary representation of a seated St Peter. The back of the shrine bears interlace and foliate patterns and the remains of an inscription which cannot be interpreted.

Altars such as these would be carried by a priest or bishop on his missionary journeys, and were apparently quite common. Symeon of Durham tells us that a wooden altar was found at the time of the mid-eleventh century translation of St Acca,

Bishop of Hexham, who died in 740. It was made of two pieces of wood fastened with silver nails and inscribed to the glory of the Trinity, St Mary and St Sophia. In the Cluny Museum in Paris is another Anglo-Saxon altar of porphyry, mounted on an oak base and bounded by strips of parcel-gilt silver [Pl. 16]. It is about 26 cm. long and has a much worn nielloed inscription round the edge (niello is the black sulphide of silver). The silver border of the porphyry face is decorated with figures: at the top is a crucifixion between the symbols of St Luke and St John; below, the symbols of St Mark and St Matthew flank an *Agnus Dei*, and on the long sides are St John and the Virgin with the two archangels, Gabriel and Raphael. The back of the altar was covered with velvet held in place by small silver plates. It is of late tenth-century date. Larger altars of undoubted pre-Conquest date do not survive in England, but we have descriptions in Anglo-Saxon literature of altar frontals, for instance the altar at Ripon, which was clothed in a rich purple textile worked with gold thread.

Also preserved in the tomb of St Cuthbert was a large ivory two-sided comb with thin teeth on one side and thicker teeth on the other. In the centre of the comb is a pierced hole and the central panel has one convex and one straight side. It is otherwise quite plain. The comb was probably made during the saint's lifetime and, although the evidence for the liturgical use of the comb at such an early date is rather slender, there can be little doubt that it was used by the celebrant in the Mass, as was occasionally the practice in the later Middle Ages.

The coffin of the Saint is a light shell of oak carved in a linear style with representations of saints and archangels. It is discussed in greater detail below (p. 150).

Probably the most interesting of St Cuthbert's relics are the vestments, particularly the stole, maniple and girdle. Inscriptions on the stole and maniple tell us that they were made to the order of Queen Ælfflaed for Bishop Frithestan. Queen Ælfflaed died before 916 and Frithestan was Bishop of Winchester from 909 to 931, so the vestments must have been made between 909 and 916. They were probably given to the shrine of St Cuthbert by Ælfflaed's stepson, King

Æthelstan, about 934, for he is recorded as having presented various gifts to the shrine including a stole, maniple and girdle. Richly embroidered on the stole are the standing figures of the sixteen prophets, separated from each other by fronds of acanthus, and set on either side of a central *Agnus Dei*; the two ends bear busts of St Thomas and St James. The maniple bore a similar design except that the central figure is the hand of God, and the flanking figures are the Pope's Sixtus II, Gregory the Great, St Lawrence and St Peter. The terminal pieces are decorated with busts of St John the Baptist and St John the Evangelist, all identified by inscriptions. The colours of these pieces of embroidery are now faded and it is difficult to distinguish them. Recent cleaning, however, has shown that as well as the gold thread which abounds, bluish-green, sage-green, delicate pinks, dark brown and dark green were all used. It was perhaps such a stole as this that we know was designed by St Dunstan for the Lady Æthelwynn to embroider a few years later. The interest of these pieces is mainly art-historical, as will be shown in a later chapter; in this context their importance lies in the fact that they are the only surviving examples of Anglo-Saxon ecclesiastical vestments.

The Trewhiddle hoard is for many reasons one of the most important finds of the whole Anglo-Saxon period. It was found in 1774 in an old mine-working at Trewhiddle, near St Austell, Cornwall, and contained, besides a number of coins which date its deposition to about 875, the animal-ornamented mounts of a drinking-horn, which ornament gives to the art of the period the name 'Trewhiddle style'. Most of the objects from the hoard are now in the British Museum. Its importance here lies in the fact that two objects of ecclesiastical use were found in the hoard, a silver scourge and a chalice. This is one of the two Anglo-Saxon chalices that survive: it is about 13 cm. high, is made of silver, and was originally collared with a beaded wire above and below the knop in the manner of many of the chalices of the period [Pl. 17]. The chalice that was found in 1104 in St Cuthbert's tomb with a paten no longer survives, but we must presume that it was similar to the gilt-bronze chalice found in the church founded by St Wilfrid at Hexham: it is small (only 6.5 cm.

Fig. 7. The Gandersheim casket. Brunswick, Herzog Anton Ulrich Museum (after Stephens)

high) and is probably a travelling chalice, perhaps one used with a portable altar like that of St Cuthbert. It is similar in shape to the Trewhiddle chalice and typologically is closely related to the great Tassilo chalice (some 26.7 cm. high), the chief treasure of the monastery of Kremsmünster in Austria [Pl. 61]. The Tassilo chalice was made for the monastery at the order of Duke Tassilo, between 777 and 788, probably by an Englishman or by a crafts- man trained in an English school.

The second ecclesiastical object found in the Trewhiddle hoard – the scourge – is unique. Scourges are otherwise known only from literature. It is made of silver wire plaited in the

Trichinopoly technique so familiar to school children, who to this day practise it under the name of 'French knitting' with the aid of a discarded cotton reel.

No crook-shaped croziers of the Anglo-Saxon period survive although Irish examples and manuscript illuminations indicate their appearance. The head of a crozier of a rather later period, however, probably from the tomb of Bishop Ranulph Flambard of Durham (died 1128), shows that they do not differ greatly from the shepherd's crook borne by modern bishops. Croziers with a T-shaped or crutch head were also used and an early eleventh-century example of such a head, made of ivory, survives from Alcester. Another similar crozier of Anglo-Saxon manufacture is in the treasury of Cologne Cathedral.

A few other pieces of church plate survive. There is, for example, a tiny jug in the British Museum which might have been used for ecclesiastical purposes. It is of cast gilt-bronze and probably dates from the early eleventh century. In the same style is a series of censer covers, one from Pershore, one from Canterbury [Pl. 79] and one from London Bridge. These three covers are cast in openwork and are square in plan with a gabled roof. The body of the censer may have been spherical and the whole object was, it seems, suspended on cords or on four thin bars which, running through the loops of the cover, allowed the top to be raised or lowered. This latter mechanism is to be seen in the illumination of a psalter, of eleventh-century date, in the British Museum.

The only surviving Anglo-Saxon altar cross is that in the treasury of the church of S. Godule in Brussels. A much more splendid example is illustrated in the eleventh-century Register of the Winchester New Minster. A small eleventh-century cross, bearing an ivory figure of Christ, in the Victoria and Albert Museum and a cross in the treasury at Maastricht are all that survive of countless such objects. A massive silver-clad cross of wood known as the cross of Rupert is in the church of Bischofshofen, near Salzburg in Austria. It is undoubtedly of insular origin and must be of eighth-century date.

Large numbers of Celtic reliquaries and shrines survive but Saxon reliquaries are rare. Two nielloed silver plates in the British Museum from a house-shaped casket probably formed part of a house-shaped shrine, of a type common throughout Europe [Pl. 18]. Similar pieces in boxwood and ivory of Anglo-Saxon manufacture are known in foreign collections, one of which, the Gandersheim casket, is of walrus ivory [Fig. 7]. Another, once in the collection of Dr Nelson, is of boxwood and bears scenes of Christian significance. A third piece, a shrine from Mortain, France, has an inscription in English runic lettering.

It is recorded that Benedict Biscop beautified the church at Monkwearmouth with sacred pictures of figures from the New Testament, while the church at Jarrow had similar pictures together with some that were intended to illustrate the connexion between the Old and the New Testaments. None of these paintings survives, and we have no idea what they looked like; but as we know of no other painting from this period other than traces of colour on tombstones and other carvings (as for instance on the famous Viking Tombstone from St Paul's churchyard in the Guildhall Museum, London, Pl. 74), we can only lament that we may no longer see, as did Leland in the sixteenth century, the brilliant painting of the cross-shaft in the church at Reculver, Kent.

The most magnificent remains of Anglo-Saxon Christianity are the manuscripts – service books and Bibles in particular – often beautifully illuminated, which survive in considerable numbers. These are of extreme importance in our understanding of Anglo-Saxon art and will be discussed in that context in another chapter. In England the art of the scribe often reached heights unequalled on the Continent and, just as the English craftsmen in Rome made church plate for the altar of St Peter's itself, so did English scribes work in the new monasteries of Germany and France. At the same time foreign craftsmen were at work in England. We have seen how glaziers and masons were brought to Northumbria by Benedict Biscop, and much later the pulpit and crucifix at Beverley were described as 'of Germanic workmanship'.

Traces of Christianity abound in secular contexts; the curse on the back of a large silver disc brooch from Sutton, Isle of Ely, bears God's name [Pl. 78]; the nose guard of the helmet from

Benty Grange bears a cross in inlaid silver; the king who was commemorated at Sutton Hoo had a pair of spoons, symbolizing a christening, inscribed with the names Saul and Paul; the ring of Queen Æthelswith bears a representation of the Lamb of God. Angels appear on an ivory panel from Winchester [Pl. 75] and the hand of God appears on coins of Edward the Elder and other Anglo-Saxon kings. The impact of Christianity on Anglo-Saxon society and its importance in everyday Saxon life are attested by these and many other similar representations of Christian symbolism.

CHAPTER THREE

The Life of the People

RURAL SETTLEMENT AND AGRICULTURE

THE Anglo-Saxon community was essentially a rural one. The economy was based on agriculture and all classes of society lived primarily on the land, either in villages or on isolated farms; only a few specialists dwelt in the towns. During the last few years it has become possible to take the first tentative steps towards a description of the kind of life the Anglo-Saxon countryman led, particularly in view of the increasing knowledge of the form of his houses and settlements. The archaeological evidence must be used with care for the settlements belong to very different periods and are scattered throughout the country on soils and in ecological circumstances which vary considerably. It is, however, tempting to try and paint a general picture on the basis of the available evidence.

There were basically four classes of society in Anglo-Saxon England; their terminology is complicated and varies from period to period, but for our purposes it is sufficient to say that the classes were, king, noble, yeoman and slave (I have carefully avoided using the technical Old English terminology); the distinction at the borders of the different classes was probably always rather blurred. It was certainly relatively easy to move from one class to another if one had the correct qualifications – in theory even kingship was not necessarily hereditary. Here I shall not discuss the refinements of the system but it might be convenient to use these broad headings for a discussion of the type of dwellings in which the people lived. Most of the sites described here are recently excavated and, as the final reports concerning them are still to appear, this discussion must be seen as incomplete and provisional.

Two royal sites are known, one from Northumbria, at Yeavering, and the other at Cheddar in the kingdom of Wessex. At Yeavering Dr Hope-Taylor has excavated the *villa regalis* mentioned by Bede in his *Ecclesiastical History* in recording the conversion of Northumbria in 627:

> So great was the fervour and desire for baptism among the people of Northumbria, that Paulinus is said to have accompanied the king and queen to the royal country seat *ad Gefrin*, and remained there 36 days constantly occupied in instructing and baptizing. ... This country seat was abandoned by the later kings who built another at ... Memlin.

The excavations revealed three main building phases: the first, of early seventh-century date, was possibly started under Æthelfrith (592–616) and enlarged under Edwin (d. 632). The second phase consisted of a rebuilding after a fire, perhaps to be associated with the ravaging of Northumbria in 632, while a third phase of rebuilding was perhaps undertaken by Oswy (654–70), after a second fire which Dr Hope-Taylor attributes to the raids of Penda, King of Mercia. To the east is a late sixth-century fort, which could be a place of refuge for the inhabitants in times of danger. The site, as it probably existed in the period of King Edwin, consisted of a number of buildings of which one massive structure was almost certainly the royal hall [Fig. 9a]; this rectangular building had two side aisles and a screened-off room at the east end. Internally it was about 27 m. long and was laid out in units based on a modified Roman foot. The walls were built of squared timbers set upright in a foundation trench, with no sill or sleeper beam. Its roof was partly supported by a series of buttresses along the side. Scattered about the site were a series of lesser halls of similar form which were presumably the houses of nobles. Dr Hope-Taylor sees one hall as a pagan temple, perhaps adapted to Christian uses after the Conversion. Another building had a sunken floor. But the most remarkable structure was undoubtedly the bank of seats, shaped like a piece cut from a circular cake, with a small platform with a screen behind it at its apex. This has been interpreted as the meeting place of an assembly. It is possible that it was the site of Paulinus's preaching to the countrymen of Bernicia.

In the succeeding phase the buildings were rebuilt on a slighter scale and a timber church was erected, around which grew an extensive cemetery.

Not far from Edinburgh, in the northernmost part of the Northumbrian kingdom – at Doon Hill, Dunbar – Dr Hope-Taylor has also excavated a building closely related to those at Yeavering within a polygonal palisaded enclosure. The hall had at one period been destroyed by fire, but rebuilt on the same pattern. Although 2.5 m. shorter than the large hall at Yeavering the halls were constructed on the same system of measurement and to the same proportions. Few details of this site have yet been published but there can be little doubt that this is a sixth-century foundation related closely in structure to that at Yeavering, but having its origin outside the purely Anglo-Saxon or Germanic tradition; for at the period at which we presumed this site to have been first inhabited this part of the world was in Celtic hands. It would seem therefore that the Yeavering type of building is a regional form and not necessarily related to the Germanic forms which are usually chosen as parallels and prototypes for Anglo-Saxon halls.

Another royal site was excavated by Mr Philip Rahtz at Cheddar, Somerset. It was a place of some importance in Anglo-Saxon England. The Witan (the National Council) met here in 941, 956 and 968, it is mentioned in the will of King Alfred and (as *sedes regalis*) in a grant of King Edwy (955–9). It has a long post-Conquest history and the most impressive building found on the site was the great twelfth-century hall.

The earliest structures at Cheddar consist of a hall with a number of ancillary buildings, which are probably of ninth-century date. The hall [Fig. 9b] was about 25 m. long, had slightly bowed sides and lateral entrances. The walls were built of closely-spaced posts about 22 cm. square, set in a trench. The posts presumably supported planking or wattle walls. Inside the hall there was an area of burnt clay (to the south of the main entrance) which may have been a hearth. There has been some discussion about a double line of posts on the western side of the hall. It has been suggested that they may have been extra supports for the roof or internal supports for a second storey building. But such an interpretation, while possible on historical grounds, seems unlikely here.

The second Anglo-Saxon phase at Cheddar consisted of a great hall [Fig. 9c] which was 19 m. long and survived with many repairs into the twelfth century. It was rectangular and had entrances in the gable-ends. Both this hall and its predecessor were associated with other smaller buildings. A small chapel, for instance, is contemporary with the later hall, as is a small rectangular building and a structure which has been tentatively interpreted as a fowl-keeper's house.

Yeavering and Cheddar are the only two royal complexes known archaeologically from the Anglo-Saxon period, although at Old Windsor excavation has revealed traces of a site of a late Anglo-Saxon palace. The royal residences at Yeavering and Cheddar may have not been very different from those of the richer members of the Anglo-Saxon society. The best indication of the wealthy landholder's residence comes, however, from the final phase of the Anglo-Saxon period (the eleventh century) from Sulgrave in Northamptonshire, where excavations by Mr Brian Davison have revealed an Anglo-Saxon hall and towered gateway, within a later embankment of roughly circular form. The excavations have not yet been completed but enough has emerged to enable us to make a number of assumptions.

The earliest building on the site was a long house of extremely sophisticated form – it apparently dates from about the year 1000 and was built of wood. The wall seems to have been planked, the uprights being set on sills. At the western end was a cobbled porch, perhaps open to the weather. Through the gable one passed into a small room and then into the main hall which had opposing doors in the lateral sides – the party wall and the opposing doors perhaps anticipating the screens passage between hall and kitchen common in the later Middle Ages. There was a central fireplace and benches along the walls. The easternmost bay was based on stone footings which remained to a height of about a metre. It seems that there may well have been at least two storeys here with an over-sailing upper floor. Axially aligned with the hall, under the tail of the rampart to the west, were the remains, in the form of substantial postholes, of a square building.

To the north of the hall was a tower, the walls of which (some 56 cm. thick) stand to a height of two metres, sufficient to reveal a metre-wide doorway with a square head. The manor of the pre-Conquest hall at Sulgrave consisted, then, of a very substantial house and a tower – exactly the qualification needed for the *thegn* of this period, according to a private compilation of the early eleventh century which runs thus:

And if a *ceorl* [a yeoman] prospered so that he possessed five hides of land of his own [a church and a kitchen], a bell and a castle gate, a seat and a special office in the king's hall, then he was henceforth entitled to the rights of *thegn* [a noble].

We have at Sulgrave then the remains of the establishment of a minor landholder of substance, later adapted by the addition of a ring-work to be a Norman knight's strong point. The presence of a tower here makes one think perhaps that the tower of the church at Earl's Barton, only a few miles away, which also stands within an earthwork, may be part of a similar complex consisting of a church and a house. So far Sulgrave is the only excavated site to indicate the settlement of a *thegn*, although the substantial remains now being excavated by Professor Barry Cunliffe within the walls of the Roman Fort of the Saxon Shore at Portchester, Hampshire, may tell a similar story.

At Portchester a fifth-century house with a sunken floor and a scatter of postholes to the north-west are the only recognizable early features. An eighth- or ninth-century rectangular building, some seven metres long, is the next main feature on the site. But the really interesting series of buildings date from the ninth to the eleventh century. The buildings [Fig. 9d] are dated by their stratigraphical situation below pits and occupation layers containing twelfth-century pottery and, because of the pottery found with them, it seems that their building history spans a longish period. Five main structures are represented on the site: building 1, a wooden building with walls of closely spaced uprights and panels of wattle and daub; building 2, a square masonry structure of two phases – probably a free-standing tower with external plaster rendering; building 3, an aisled hall about 13 m. long; building 4, another rectangular hall about 10 m. long; and building 5, yet another rectangular hall.

Professor Cunliffe has interpreted the sequence on the site as follows: buildings 1, 3 and 5 and the early phase of building 2 belong to one period. In a second period building 3 was demolished and a cemetery of some eighteen burials was allowed to spread over the site. At the same time the west end of building 1 was rebuilt, building 4 was erected and building 5 was possibly reconstructed. The third phase encompasses the reconstruction of the tower.

The history of Portchester is extremely complicated and any interpretation of these remains must therefore be tentative, as only a small part of a large fortified area has been excavated. Domesday Book records that there was a hall on the site. It was certainly taken into royal control as a fortified place against the Vikings in 902 and a Norman castle was built here after the Conquest; it is not mentioned until 1153, but was probably constructed about 1100. The house and building complex may not, therefore, certainly be interpreted as a *thegn*'s dwelling, although the correspondence with the situation at Sulgrave is not without significance. We cannot really differentiate the functions of the buildings, although we seem to have the tower, the church and the hall of the man who might be considered a *thegn*.

Kings, earls and *thegns*; all these had their houses and lands, but most of the people in Anglo-Saxon England lived as *ceorls*, or freemen, or as bondmen on the land. It was during the Anglo-Saxon period that the village became an important element in the English landscape and the archaeologists' attempts to find evidence for such settlements must now be discussed. Here the picture is, for various reasons, unsatisfactory. Firstly, many of the villages founded during the Anglo-Saxon period survive to-day under modern settlements. Secondly, the excavation of a large settlement is a very expensive procedure and one which is difficult to finance. Thirdly, such excavations take time and as yet we have no completely recorded village excavation in England, although patterns are beginning to emerge.

There is no evidence, either archaeological or historical, for the survival of the Roman villa system into the Anglo-Saxon period. In this respect the province of Britannia is entirely different from Gaul, for in south and central France there is adequate evidence of the continuity of villa sites – evidence, for example, in the form of place names. This is not the case in England. Few non-urban place names in England go back to the Roman period: most are of Anglo-Saxon origin and show that it was the Anglo-Saxons, not the Romans, who formed the pattern of settlement of the English countryside. At no villa site so far excavated in England has any important trace of immediate post-Roman settlement survived, although there are traces of people who might be distinguished as *laeti* settling near Roman settlements. We shall discuss one such case at Mucking, Essex, shortly. Mr Rivet has expressed the probable reason for this continuity succinctly:

It has often been remarked that no case is known where Saxons occupied a Roman villa. In part this was no doubt due to their social organisation, based on the great hall, to which the typical villa was totally unsuited. ... But it is probable that the over-riding reason was that by the time of the main Saxon settlement the villas, cut off from their economic and social basis, had already tumbled to ruin.

The newcomers were forced to introduce a new economic system into the country, one to which they were accustomed. In so doing they largely shaped the English countryside as we know it today.

As we investigate more and more Anglo-Saxon settlement sites in England the picture of a village composed of a fairly large number of small huts (6 m. long) with sunken floors becomes clearer. Earlier excavations at Sutton Courtenay and Cassington had already suggested that this was the case, although Dr Radford, arguing from the parallels at Warendorf in Westphalia, thought that the village would consist of small sunken-floored huts together with long hall-houses. So far nothing quite like Warendorf has, however, been found in England and we must assume that the poorest members of Anglo-Saxon society lived in villages composed of small huts with sunken floors, and only rarely – as at Eynsham, Oxfordshire, and West Stow, Suffolk – have hall-houses been found in association with such huts on Anglo-Saxon village sites. They have been found together in towns – but that is a completely different matter. I suggest that the normal village was controlled by a man of noble rank who frequently lived at some distance from the agricultural settlement.

Among the most important sites at present being excavated in England is that at Mucking, Essex, a site with a commanding position over a bend in the Thames estuary. No plan of this site has yet been produced, but it is known that more than eighty sunken-floored huts have been excavated there, and that another thirty may well remain to be examined. The houses lie on the facing slope of the 30 m. Thames gravel-terrace. The normal hut is about 4 m. long and 3 m. across, with a deep posthole at either end of the long axis. They are pretty miserable structures, but their floors have accumulated a large amount of material which shows that they date from the period before the end of Roman Britain to the seventh century. Such a date is also suggested by the closely associated cemetery, some of the graves of which have produced some very rich material, particularly a sub-Roman buckle-set, decorated in the 'quoit-brooch' style (see p. 132f.). Finds are rich and the pottery is particularly interesting. Dr Myres in discussing the pottery of the settlement area writes 'These [first twenty] huts have already produced between them more pieces to which a date in the decades before and after AD 400 must be assigned than any other domestic site in England, more indeed than are known at present from all the other recognized domestic sites of the pagan Anglo-Saxon period in this country put together.' What are even more interesting are the close parallels between this pottery and the Germanic pottery of the late fourth and early fifth centuries.

It is significant that this pottery occurs on the Continent in association with material which is alleged to have belonged to the Germanic *laeti*, who served with the Romans at the end of the fourth and the beginning of the fifth centuries, and Dr Myres has suggested that the earliest Germanic settlers at Mucking may have been *laeti*. The position of this settlement overlooking the Thames would help to control the approaches to

Roman London. It was almost at this point of the river that, from the sixteenth century onwards, a series of forts was built for a similar purpose to control the same reaches with artillery. Dr Myres suggests that a para-military settlement at Mucking lasted until the middle of the fifth century when it grew into a normal Anglo-Saxon village.

The form of the settlement is interesting. There are no street lines and the houses are scattered, almost casually, over a wide area; perhaps, as about a dozen of the huts are dug next to Roman field boundaries, they had some relation to an existing field system. The site extends over a considerable area and connects with another site, some 500 metres away, which was excavated in 1955 by Mr Kenneth Barton, a site which is referred to in the literature as Linford. This then was obviously a considerable settlement and lasted on the same site for perhaps 250 years. At the moment it is of course difficult to say what was the size, and the excavator, Mrs Jones, actually goes so far as to suggest that these mean huts may be peripheral to a main settlement to the south-east. I am not entirely happy about this suggestion, but one must obviously suspend judgement until the excavation is finished.

The huts revealed a body of evidence of semi-industrial activity, such as horn-working, plumbing and weaving, but most of the finds are domestic in character, including a great deal of coarse, hand-made, 'grass-tempered' pottery.

Huts with sunken floors are found throughout southern England; they seem to have been as common here as they were on the Continent and there is little point in denying that they were the normal type of house of the poorer classes of society. There is sufficient evidence on the Continent to show that the interpretation of them as exclusively industrial buildings is wrong, although some of them were certainly used for industrial or semi-industrial purposes. Settlements are, however, known in this country where the only structures are rectangular houses – I would give as an example Maxey, Northamptonshire, where a number of rectangular structures were traced in close proximity to each other. This might possibly be a village or an example of the farm complex of a seventh-century nobleman.

One specific type of house deserves to be mentioned: the house with the curved sides – a type which is of a form found throughout Germanic Europe [Fig. 8a]. The clearest picture we have of these houses in England rests on the evidence of the hogbacked tombstones, which are of tenth- or eleventh-century date and occur in Viking contexts in the north of England. Such tombstones indicate that the roofs of such houses were curved,

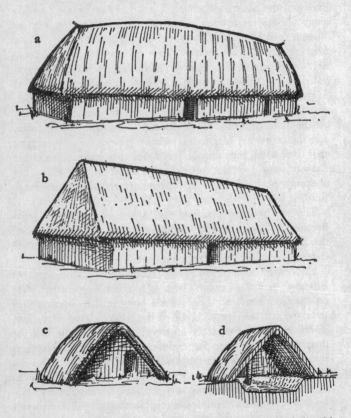

Fig. 8. Reconstructions of Anglo-Saxon houses: (a) the hall with bowed sides from Cheddar; (b) long house from Thetford; (c) hut with sunken floor from Thetford; (d) section through c

as were their walls. They also indicate that they were covered with slabs of stone, tiles, or even with wooden plates or shingles (of a type known from Anglo-Saxon excavations in Winchester). The walls were apparently of plaited wattle between posts. The plan of such houses is well known in contemporary Danish Viking encampments, but have a Continental history which extends back to the fifth century. Such houses occur at Buckden, Hunts, Cheddar [Figs. 8a, 9b] and at Portchester [Fig. 9d]; they are also said to have occurred in towns such as Thetford. Their function differed not at all from the normal rectangular house.

Parallels abroad and literary description suggest that all the main business of life was carried on in the hall – eating, sleeping, entertaining. A very rich man might have separate sleeping quarters as, sometimes, did the women; but such separate buildings were not universal.

Work on the village in the countryside is just beginning. Mr Fowler has started to investigate at Fyfield Down the relationships of field and parish boundaries to Anglo-Saxon land utilization. The problem is complicated and one that will take many years to solve. The difficulties of the problem are self-evident. It is one thing to examine a village in Wiltshire, but it is an entirely different matter to try and apply the knowledge gained there to settlements in different regions, on the gravels of the Thames Valley or on the millstone grits of the Pennines. Ultimately, however, a method of examining this problem may be worked out and this, combined with an examination of traces of grain and an analysis of animal bones, will help to bring alive a good deal of the rural economy of the Anglo-Saxons.

Certain facts are already available and can be simply stated. The most common cereals were barley, oats and wheat. Flax was grown for cloth-making and woad for dyeing. Fruit and nuts were probably gathered from the forest, and Parain has suggested that a few rough fruit trees were even planted deliberately on the edge of the forest. Tools were needed for these pursuits, but few have survived.

No plough, and only a few plough-shares (as, for example, from Thetford and Westly Waterless, Cambs.), are known to

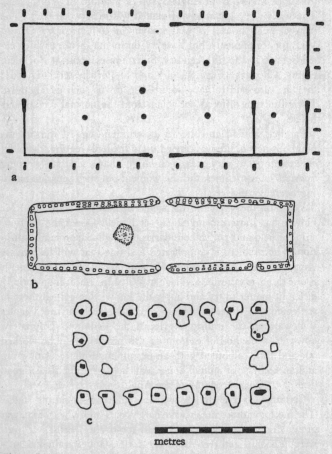

Fig. 9. (a) Plan of a king's hall at Yeavering (after Hope-Taylor); (b) Plan of 'boat-shaped' hall from Cheddar (after Rahtz); (c) The twelfth-century state of the second great hall at Cheddar (after Rahtz); (d) Provisional plan of the layout of the late Anglo-Saxon building complex at Portchester (after Cunliffe)

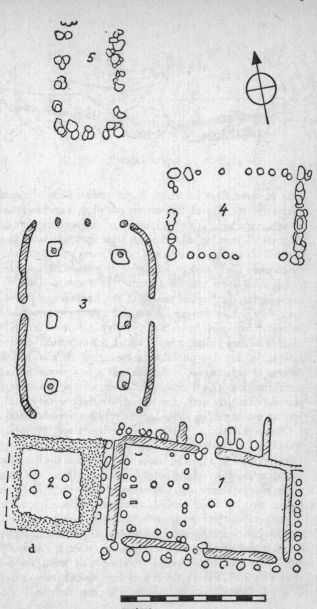

metres

Fig. 10a. Plough, from the Bayeux Tapestry

have survived from the Anglo-Saxon period. From the manuscripts and the Bayeux tapestry we can glean a certain amount
of evidence which, however, must be treated with extreme care.
An artist illuminating a manuscript would not necessarily go out
in the fields and look at a plough before he drew it: he would be
much more likely to copy a drawing from another manuscript,
which may itself have been painted in Padua or Paris. The
evidence for the English plough of the Anglo-Saxon period is,
then, very slender, but certain suggestions as to its structure can
be made [Fig. 10a]. It was a fairly heavy implement drawn by a
number of oxen; it had a heavy wheel, but no mould-board; the
furrow was cut and turned by a coulter which was shifted at
the end of each furrow, so that the next furrow would lie in the
same direction. The field would then be harrowed with an implement that may well have looked like the one shown in the
Bayeux tapestry [Fig. 10b], and the seed scattered broadcast.

Certain harvesting implements survive. Four scythe-blades
were found at Hurbuck in County Durham, in a hoard of Anglo-
Saxon tools [Fig. 11]. The blades were bound to the handle and
the upturned point of the tang, which can still be seen on one
of the Hurbuck examples, was hammered into the haft to give it
greater security. These scythe-blades bear a striking resemblance
to scythes illustrated in manuscripts. Sickles have been found in
two English Viking graves. Bill-hooks and pitch-forks are illustrated in the manuscripts [Fig. 12], but none is known from
Anglo-Saxon contexts. Spades were made of wood and were
shod with iron [Fig. 13]. A few of these shoes have been found
in archaeological contexts, including the example from Sandtun,

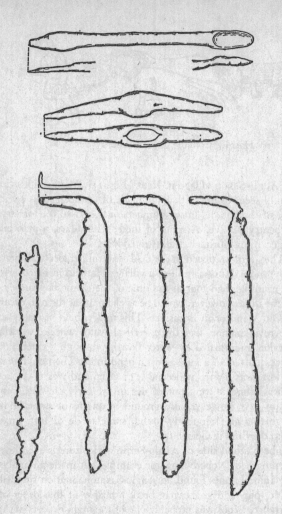

Fig. 11. Hoard of tools from Hurbuck, Co. Durham, including scythe blades, axes, adzes, an auger and a small pick. London, British Museum

Fig. 10b. Harrow, from the Bayeux Tapestry

an Anglo-Saxon village in Kent [Fig. 14]. Manuscript evidence would seem to imply that the blade of the spade was set at one side of the handle. Large numbers of axes used for forestry and carpentry survive. A series of these, with adzes, a pick and an auger, from Hurbuck, is illustrated here.

The grain produced in the fields was milled locally. There was often more than one mill in a village; Hatfield in Hertfordshire, for example, had four at the time of the Domesday survey. Not all the mills, however, would be as elaborate as the mill excavated at Old Windsor in Berkshire. This mill, which probably served the royal manor, had three vertical water wheels, working in parallel and turned by water flowing through a ditch dug for three-quarters of a mile across a bend in the Thames. The ditch, or leet, was 6.5 m. wide and 4 m. deep and was re-cut several times before it went out of use in the early eleventh century. Grain was, however, also ground in querns of stone of which fragments are frequently found, some made of lava imported from the Eifel in Germany.

The pastoral side of Anglo-Saxon agriculture is even less well documented. Nobody has, for example, yet made an analysis of the animal bones found on Anglo-Saxon habitation sites. Sheep, cattle, pigs and goats were bred, probably in that order of importance. Wool was probably one of the main exports of Anglo-Saxon England and the cloth industry seems to have been extensive; all that survives in the archaeological record, however, beside the odd sheep-bone, is a few pairs of shears and a tool found at Sutton Courtenay, which might have been used for carding wool. Sheep and cattle were, of course, also kept for

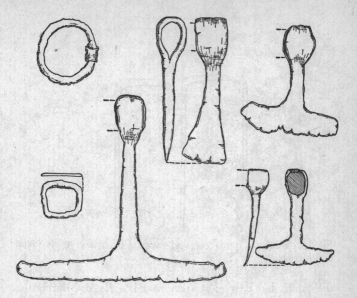

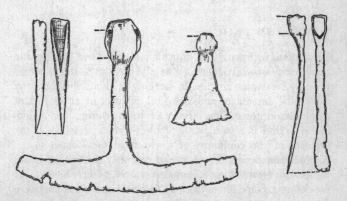

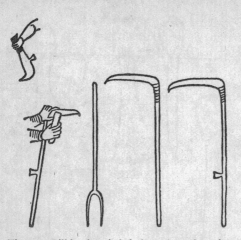

Fig. 12. Bill-hook, pitch-fork and scythes, from late Anglo-Saxon manuscripts

their milk and their meat: they would be fattened during the summer and the least promising beasts would be slaughtered in the autumn, the meat being preserved by salting or drying. Only the strongest cattle would be kept through the winter. Horses were luxury animals but certainly existed in some numbers and were used for draught as well as for riding.

TOWNS AND TRADE

Excavation in towns is a difficult and expensive process and opportunities to investigate substantial areas of a single period town by excavation are rare. In fact only at Thetford is there any substantial amount of archaeological evidence of an important Anglo-Saxon town. The history of towns during the Anglo-Saxon period is riddled with problems, chief of which is the problem of the continuity of towns from the Roman to the Anglo-Saxon period. There are no definitely continuous urban institutions recorded in the historical sources, as there are in Gaul for example. Some towns (such as Silchester and Wroxeter) were

certainly deserted by all but a handful of
poor squatters soon after the withdrawal
of the Romans from the province. On
the other hand there is no evidence that
the towns immediately fell into decay
when the Romans left. Germanus, for
example, visited Verulamium in 429 and
found a reasonably constructed administration; while Paulinus, visiting
Lincoln in 627, was met by a man
described as *praefectus* (a position im-
plying some municipal organization).
But there can be little doubt that most
towns began to decay as the Roman
economic system creaked to a standstill.
This is splendidly illustrated by the fact
that King Offa, in the late eighth
century, gave the deserted ruins of Verulamium as a gift to the abbey founded

Fig. 13. Man using
spade; notice the sug-
gestion of a shoe at its
point (after the Bayeux
Tapestry)

on the other side of the river to the memory of the British proto-
martyr, St Alban.

Canterbury was certainly one of the towns which survived,
albeit miserably, with its name changed from Durovernum. Ex-

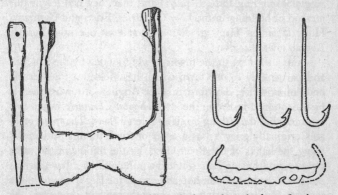

Fig. 14. Fish-hooks, draw-knife and shoe of spade from Sandtun,
Kent. London, British Museum

cavations here in 1960 produced six small sunken-floored huts of the fifth century, set some 10m. back from the Roman street but on line with it. Canterbury quickly became an important Anglo-Saxon town and the capital of the Kentish people. There was still derelict Roman property, however, in Canterbury in the 590s when Augustine came there, for he found the queen's chaplain using an old Roman church, but the stereotyped town plan of Roman Canterbury did not develop into the town plan of the medieval period, although some of the street lines were obviously retained. The same is true, for example, of York, although there was an initial attempt to use the Roman building line. This has recently been demonstrated by excavations within the minster at York, where it appears that the early archiepiscopal church – the church known to Alcuin – may have been situated in part of the headquarters building of the Roman city, or at least aligned on the walls of that building (unlike its Romanesque successor).

Dorchester-on-Thames, like Canterbury, has also produced early sunken-floored huts. Just outside the walls of the Roman town is a cemetery which has produced graves of Germanic *laeti*. The huts within the walls are possibly contemporary with these graves and one is tempted to suggest that houses of this sort were the normal houses of the mercenary Germanic settlers of early Anglo-Saxon England (cf. p. 71) and that they had learnt this method of building in the Low Countries, Frisia and Germany. Huts of similar form are found in at least one other former Roman town, London.

Let us turn next to the towns newly founded by the English, and particularly to one town which has yielded a considerable body of evidence, Thetford in East Anglia – a town which is first mentioned in 870 in the *Anglo-Saxon Chronicle*, when it is recorded that the Viking armies wintered there. The town probably originally grew up as a series of small trading settlements along the banks of the River Ouse. By the middle of the tenth century, under King Edgar, it had a mint, and for a few glorious years was the seat of a bishop and one of the largest towns in the country (p. 85). During the eleventh century, however, the population of Thetford – at that time the second largest town in

East Anglia – moved across the river and built a new town on the northern bank. Excavations between 1948 and 1952 by Group Captain Knocker on the ancient south bank site produced a few houses, which more recent excavators have interpreted as a small peripheral industrial area, straggling along the cobbled roads near the town defences. More recently excavations just south of the river bank, in a more important area of the town, have been carried out by Mr Brian Davison.

The earliest Anglo-Saxon features on the site are four huts with sunken floors which vary in length between 3·5 and 6 metres. The roof was supported by single uprights in the centre of the gable ends. One hut had a fireplace. The huts perhaps belong to the pagan Anglo-Saxon period. They stand in isolation and bear no obvious relation to other neighbouring features of the site. There are no finds from the seventh and eighth centuries. But, dating from the ninth to twelfth centuries, are a number of rectangular buildings, of which the largest is some 36 m. in length. A number of other rectangular buildings were also excavated; they were smaller, but two had cellars (one with a mortared floor).

A little to the south of the main site, just within the defences, were a number of eleventh-century kilns which produced the distinctive hard, grey, Thetford pottery. The kilns were grouped in the centre of a yard (with apparently no subsidiary buildings or sheds around them) and took various forms, of which the most astonishing was a trefoil battery of three kilns served from a single stoking-pit. The ovens are formed of clay-lined pits between 2 and 3 m. in length. During firing the pots were supported by a series of clay arches and, from a number of collapsed kilns found on the site, it seems that only between twenty and fifty pots were stacked in a kiln at one firing.

Thetford grew casually as a town; there is no apparent alignment on a street grid or on any other kind of plan. There seems to have been some zoning of industries, but even in the rather large area excavated it is impossible to generalize, as we may only be dealing with a relatively rich quarter. The best evidence of town planning in the late Anglo-Saxon period occurs at Lydford, Devon, and North Elmham, Norfolk, where there seems to be some evidence of a systematic layout of an Anglo-Saxon town along the lines of the main street; but these were very small communities.

Archaeology and the historical sources confirm the impression that already before the Viking invasion some towns were flourishing centres of trade and mutual protection. Such towns were Rochester, Canterbury, Carlisle, Thetford, Winchester, Dorchester, Lincoln, Hamwih (the early port of Southampton) and, of course, London, which was described by Bede in the early eighth century as a market for many peoples coming by land and sea. Nevertheless, the great development in English town life came in and after the reign of Alfred in the late ninth century. The need to protect the country against Danish attack led to the foundation of a series of fortified boroughs.

The archaeological investigation of the towns of this period has been largely concentrated on their defences. This is particularly true of one of the greatest of Alfred's foundations, Wallingford, where Mr Brooks has been excavating the embanked fortifications of the Alfredian town, and similar evidence has been uncovered at Wareham, Dorset, and Lydford, Devon. At Hereford, likewise, excavation of the town walls has also produced a series of successive Anglo-Saxon ramparts. The sequence is complex and reflects the attention paid to the duty of fortification in early medieval documents. The boroughs created by Alfred and his successors were military in purpose, but, although they were organized as strong points, their origins need not have been military: some were already thriving towns, some markets, some merely royal manors. They were created by the king, but economic circumstances decided their fate. Some survived and grew into towns which still prosper; some faded and were lost, and the historians and philologists today quarrel over their location – as for example over the identity of the borough of *Sceaftesege* which has recently been tentatively identified as Sashes, on the Thames near Cookham.

One borough was very strongly fortified – the post-Alfredian town at South Cadbury, Somerset. This town was set within the ramparts of an Early Iron Age hill-fort and for a long time, since the sixteenth century at least, the site has been equated with that of the Camelot of the semi-legendary King Arthur. Despite a few finds of the Arthurian period there is as yet no substantial evidence that this was an early Anglo-Saxon royal site, but in the early eleventh century it was fortified by Æthelred and may well have been razed by his successor, Cnut, for the minting of coins ceased here in Cnut's reign. Investigation of the south-western entrance of the late Anglo-Saxon town has revealed traces of the gateway. It was 3.3 m. wide and 9 m. deep, the doors pivoted on sockets cut in stone and the responds of the doorway continued in the same Ham stone up to the head of the door. The main face of the wall was built up of limestone slabs bedded in a hard mortar.

From the Domesday Book historians have calculated, in a conservative fashion, the population figures for some of the Anglo-Saxon towns. The following are Professor Loyn's estimates for 1066: London (for which no real figures are available) 12,000, York 8,000, Norwich and Lincoln 5,000 each, Thetford 4,000, Oxford 3,500 and Colchester 2,000. These were important towns but we cannot generalize about them on the basis of the present archaeological evidence, despite the preliminary results of the Thetford excavations.

The town served two primary functions in the Anglo-Saxon period; first as a defence and administrative centre, and secondly as a market and economic centre. The defences of Wareham illustrate the former function to perfection; within these walls men could live in comparative safety in the troubled periods when pirates and raiders were abroad. From the *Anglo-Saxon Chronicle* we have an interesting picture of the native inhabitants of Winchester in 1006, protected by the town's fortifications, watching from a distance the Viking host marching with their booty to the sea. Not only would the inhabitants of a town benefit from its fortifications but the people from the surrounding countryside would be able to take refuge there in time of trouble. The fortification of thirty-one Wessex towns in the time of King Alfred means, as Sir Frank Stenton long ago pointed out, that in Wessex no village was more than twenty miles away from a fortified centre.

But it is the economic function of the town that leaves most trace in the archaeological record. Exotic materials – precious stones, glass, bronzes, mill-stones, silver vessels, coins and many other objects – found in Anglo-Saxon contexts are indicative of the primary function of a town: trade. The towns were not only markets for agricultural produce from the surrounding countryside, they served also as markets for goods from abroad. Although most of the trade must have been carried out by means of barter, the presence of a coinage of extremely high standard indicates a medium of trade more normal to civilized communities.

It was not until the late seventh century that the first Anglo-Saxon coins were struck. The hoard from Crondall in Hampshire, deposited about 670, is particularly important in this context. It contained, besides two pieces of jewellery, 101 gold coins, of which seventy-three are some of the earliest surviving Anglo-Saxon imitations of Roman and Merovingian coins. Gold was not destined to remain the metal of currency for very long; it was to be replaced by silver, but the struggle to retain the gold standard is reflected in a number of coins struck in electrum (an alloy of gold and silver). By the early eighth century, however, the Anglo-Saxons had adopted the silver coinage which was to remain the basis of all trade until the fourteenth century.

The earliest silver coins were, despite various attempts to maintain a high standard, often degenerate and debased in weight and legend. But about 780 Offa had taken over from Kent a new coin, the penny, which became of increasing influence in the succeeding years. Towards the end of his reign Offa standardized the weight of the penny at twenty-two grains and it rarely dropped below this figure for nearly five hundred years.

The English coinage was essentially a royal institution, although the archbishops of Canterbury and York were allowed to strike their own coins. The actual coining, however, was done in many provincial centres, presumably under the control of the reeve or other royal official. The privilege of striking coins was farmed out to a professional moneyer, whose name usually appears on the reverse of the coin. The penalties for debasing the coinage were extremely heavy and were presumably strictly enforced, for base coin is rarely found. It has already been noted that, in Edgar's reign and in the succeeding reigns, the coinage was called in and reissued at regular intervals. Similarly all foreign money which came into the country in the last two centuries of the Anglo-Saxon period was melted down and re-struck. In this way the king could retain the standard of his coinage with no cost to himself, for the moneyer would buy coins for reminting by weight and not by face value. This interest of the Anglo-Saxon kings in keeping up the standard of the currency made English coinage a recognized medium of exchange from the Balkans to Scandinavia.

We have already mentioned a few of the more exotic imported materials which have been found in Anglo-Saxon contexts, and which must have reached this country by way of trade. This trade was carried on by people of all countries, but three nations seem to have dominated the trade of Europe for long periods of time – the Frisians, the Jews and the Arabs. The Frisians, who lived on the fertile shore of Holland, practically controlled the trade of Northern Europe. They were a maritime people who had colonies in London and York and travelled between the great Baltic ports of the Viking Age, Birka, Hedeby and Sciringesheal, carrying thither Rhenish wine, English and Frankish weapons, hunting dogs, oriental silks and English cloth, to barter for ropes, amber, furs – fox, beaver, sable and ermine – and slaves. The Jews and the Arabs controlled the trade in Southern Europe, Asia and Africa. Ibn Horradadbeh describes one Jewish merchant thus: 'This merchant spoke the Arabic, Persian, Latin, French, Spanish and Slav languages. He travelled from the Occident to the Orient, sometimes by land and sometimes by sea. From the West he took eunuchs, women slaves, boys, brocade, beaver-skins, marten-pelts, other furs and swords.' He started in Western Europe (in the Frankish lands) by the Western Sea and travelled by sea to al-Farama (Pelusium in Egypt); then, changing his mode of transport on various occasions, he travelled by way of Arabia to India and China. On his return journey 'he bore with him muscat, aloes, camphor, cinnamon and other products of the East and returned with them to Constantinople'. This was but one of a number of journeys of like character made by this man; it reminds us that the international trade of Europe in the Dark Ages was extensive and that the trade connexions of many of the merchants of this period would have put many a modern business house to shame.

But the Frisians, Arabs and Jews were not the only merchants: Anglo-Saxons were also trading with the Continent: 'I go on board my ship', says the merchant in Ælfric's *Colloquy*, 'with my freight and row over the regions of the sea, and sell my goods and buy precious things which are not produced in this land, and I bring it hither to you with great danger over the sea and sometimes I suffer shipwreck with the loss of all my goods, barely escaping with my life.' He describes the goods he brings back,

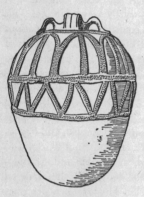

Fig. 15. *Relief-band amphora* from the Rhineland. Fragments of vessels of this type appear in English contexts. Scale about 1/12.

'purple and silk, precious gems and gold, rare garments and spices, wine and oil, ivory and brass, copper and tin, sulphur and glass and suchlike things ...' English merchants traded hunting-dogs, furs, silver, linen, slaves, horses and weapons with Italy, and entered into trade agreements with the kings of Lombardy. The merchant bought and sold where and when he could; the type of cargo he carried with him was conditioned only by economic considerations. He had to contend with tolls and taxes, embargoes and customs officials; there is ample evidence of all these mercantile hazards in the documentary sources, while more direct piracy was also a very present danger, particularly in the Viking Age.

The trade in perishable goods, which formed such an important part of the Anglo-Saxon mercantile system, is reflected in certain instances in the archaeological material. While we cannot hope to trace archaeologically the chief exports of Anglo-Saxon England – wool and cloth – certain imports have left their mark. The occurrence of Continental pottery in England has already been mentioned. From the seventh century onwards we have evidence that pottery was imported from the Continent, which must presumably be associated with the German wine trade. The great *relief-band amphorae* [Fig. 15], some of them three or four feet in height, can have been used for no other purpose than transporting wine. The wooden barrels which are depicted on the Bayeux tapestry [Fig. 16] and which presumably contained French wine have not left any trace in the pre-Conquest archaeological material, although remains of an immediately post-Conquest example have been found at Pevensey Castle.

The Eastern trade is reflected in such objects as the Egyptian glass found in an Anglo-Saxon grave in Sussex. Other fragments of Eastern glass in the Christian Anglo-Saxon period come from London, Chichester, Yorkshire and Fife. Also from the East are bronze bowls imported from Alexandria, garnets possibly from India, and cowrie shells from the Indian Ocean, which tell us that mercantile contacts with the Orient were not casual. But apart from the occasional fragments of Oriental silk, we have no traces of spices and dyes and other perishable goods which the East could provide for the peripheral islands of the world.

TRANSPORT

One of the chief legacies of Rome was a system of roads, built so that Roman armies and merchandise could move quickly about the country. These well-constructed roads were used by the Anglo-Saxons in their ordinary day-to-day business. There can be little doubt that they deteriorated during the Anglo-Saxon period, but the volume of traffic was by no means as heavy as

Fig. 16. Wagon, containing a barrel, drawn by two men. The Bayeux Tapestry

that in later medieval, Tudor and Stuart times, and the roads must have been in fairly good condition. The speed with which armies moved across country adequately reflects the condition of the roads.

The Anglo-Saxons apparently thought of the roads not, as the Romans had done, as a system of trunk communications, but as a means of communication between market towns. Small tracks were developed from the newly-founded villages linking the village directly with the nearest town or with the nearest stretch of made road. Along the roads passed messengers and parties of clerics, royal officials and pilgrims, pack-animals and carts carrying merchandise, and the baggage train of the royal court as it moved from centre to centre.

There is but little archaeological trace of the means of transport. Pieces of horse-harness are all that survive. No traces of the carts that figure in the manuscripts and in the Bayeux tapestry [Fig. 16] remain. Both two- and four-wheeled carts are represented in the manuscript sources and they appear to have been drawn by men as well as by draught animals. Farm carts had bodies of light staves (and perhaps of wickerwork). The wheels were spoked and made up of composite felloes. Travelling wagons, which would make longer journeys, were probably more substantially built and roofed with leather.

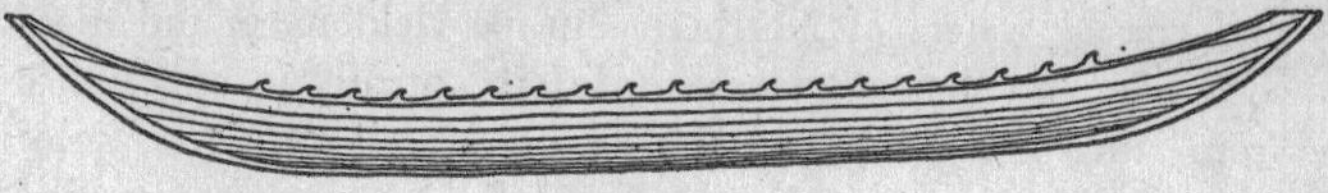

Fig. 17. The Sutton Hoo ship reconstructed

Whenever possible, however, merchandise was transported by water. This was quicker, less physically exhausting, and cheaper. The northern European practice of boat burial, to which we have already referred, has preserved for us the plans of three boats. They all date from the seventh century and were all three found in Suffolk – one at Snape and two at Sutton Hoo. They were all rowing-boats: the largest and most complete example was that found at Sutton Hoo in 1939 [Fig. 17]. The timbers of this boat had decayed until nearly all the actual body of the wood had disappeared, but the excavators skilfully isolated the marks left in the soil by the decaying wood and the iron clench nails which fastened the strakes to each other, and were able to plan and photograph the complete vessel. The ship was about 29 m. long and 4·25 m. in the beam; the prow rose to a height of at least 3·8 m. above the level of the keel-plank amidships. It was a rowing-boat and, when lightly loaded, would have drawn about two feet of water. There were nine strakes on each quarter. To the wash strake, or gunwale strake, were attached thorn-shaped rowlocks. The keel was little more than a thickened plank. The ship was strengthened with twenty-six ribs, which were nailed only at their ends, presumably being lashed to cleats on the strakes. There was no trace of the steering oar. The ship was already of some age when it was buried, as there are traces of repairs.

Anglo-Saxon sailing ships have not been found, but they were almost certainly known before we have written record of them in the ninth century. A Roman sailing ship is recorded from London and there is Continental evidence of sailing ships in northern waters in the pagan Anglo-Saxon period. The Vikings certainly came to England in the square-sailed, single-masted ships which have become a symbol of the Scandinavian raiders. Our knowledge of these vessels grows year by year as the graves and coastal waters of Northern Europe yield more and more evidence, and they cannot have differed greatly in appearance from their Anglo-Saxon contemporaries. That there were different forms of ships in the North Sea is, however, implied by a passage in the *Anglo-Saxon Chronicle* under the year 896: 'Then King Alfred had long ships built to oppose the Danish warships. They were almost twice as long as the others. Some had sixty oars, some more. They were both swifter and steadier and also higher than the others. They were built neither on the Frisian or on the Danish pattern, but as it seemed to him himself that they could be most useful.'

Small boats of the Anglo-Saxon period have not been found in England. Some must have been miniature editions of sea-going vessels, but we must presume that skin boats and coracles were also used by the fishermen who lost their fish-hooks at Sandtun in Kent [Fig. 14].

DRESS AND PERSONAL ORNAMENT

No fragment of ordinary Anglo-Saxon dress of more than a few square inches in size survives. Our knowledge of dress has therefore to be built up on the evidence of a few clothes found on the Continent, on pictorial evidence and on literary sources. The literary sources provide us with precious little information, and that of the most casual sort: an English missionary bishop, for example, freezing as a result of a German winter, sends home a *cri de cœur* for a new cloak. Another cleric, Alcuin, sends to a friend on the Continent for garments and hoods of goat-hair. In Frankish sources we have fuller descriptions of dress. Charlemagne, for example, took a patriotic pride in dressing in the native costume of the Franks. Einhard tells us that he wore some sort of linen combinations beneath his trousers and a woollen three-quarter-length tunic, trimmed with silk and belted at the waist. His shoes, which were buckled over his feet, had bands attached to them, with which he cross-gartered his legs. He wore a fur cape, which appears to have been fairly short but covered both the front and the back of his body. Over all this he

Fig. 18. Clothes of the rich portrayed in eleventh-century manuscripts

wore a long, flowing mantle, fastened at the shoulder by a brooch.

Dress of more or less this same form seems to have been worn generally in Western and Northern Europe from the Roman period to the Conquest, by all but the richer members of society.

The clothes described by Einhard correspond in many details to those found on the Continent (some of which may be as much as four hundred years earlier in date) as well as to clothes portrayed on objects of Anglo-Saxon origin, as for example [Pl. 56] on the Franks Casket (dated *c.* 700) and in manuscripts of the tenth and eleventh centuries [Fig. 18]. Basically men's clothes would consist of cross-gartered trousers or stockings, a short tunic, a cloak fastened at the shoulder by a brooch, pin or thorn, and (at certain periods at least) a hood. Some men apparently went bare-legged. The clothes could vary considerably in fabric and in design, and among the richer members of society could be dyed the most brilliant colours. The care of the hair was important and in at least two letters an Anglo-Saxon is admonished against trimming his hair in a 'Danish' fashion, perhaps with a bare neck.

The learned cleric, Aldhelm, fulminating against the immodest dress affected by certain nuns, gives us a picture of dress in the late seventh century:

In both sexes this kind of costume consists of an undergarment of the finest cloth, a red or blue tunic, a head-dress and sleeves with silk borders; their shoes are adorned with red dyed skins; the locks on their temples and foreheads are crimped by the curlers. In the place of dark head coverings they wear white and coloured veils which hang down richly to the feet and are held in place by ribbons [*vittae*] sewn on to them. Finger-nails are sharpened like hawks' talons . . .

Of all these clothes the only survivors are the braided ribbons (*vittae*) which have been found in a number of the richer Anglo-Saxon women's burials. These are bands of fine cloth and gold thread woven by tablet weaving (a method also used to produce braided bands which were popularly used as edging to cloaks and at the cuffs).

It is difficult, however, to say anything about female fashion in the Anglo-Saxon period. Mrs Hawkes has suggested that the richer members of society changed to a Mediterranean style of dress with the coming of Christianity, a thesis which rests on new modes of wearing jewellery in the seventh century, when one brooch, not two, is found in the graves of the richer members of society. This was the period of the rich disc brooch (e.g. Pl. 35). From the tenth century onwards we have a fairly good idea of the appearance of the clothes of both men and women from such manuscript drawings as those depicted in Fig. 18 and Pl. 70. But for earlier periods it is perhaps wiser not to speculate.

The commonest fabric was wool, which even at this period must have been of great importance to the English economy. Fragments of wool survive quite frequently and vary from a very fine quality, rather like flannel, to coarse tweed-like materials. Woollen cloth, and indeed linen, was woven on a warp-weighted loom. The loom took the form of a rectangular upright frame which leant against the wall of a house, the warps being kept taut by baked clay rings tied to the end. These weights are the only clue we have to the form of the loom and are frequently found on Anglo-Saxon sites. Sometimes, when a hut has been burnt down, a line of loom-weights is found on the floor of the hut. Indeed, the occurrence of loom weights in houses with sunken floors for a long time convinced archaeologists that such huts were frequently used for weaving only. These huts were, however, ordinary dwellings and the ubiquitous nature of the finds of loom weights demonstrates, rather, the great importance and universality of weaving in rural Anglo-Saxon communities.

Silk was also used by the rich as cloth and for embroidery, goat's-hair blankets have already been mentioned, and linen must have been quite common. Perhaps the most remarkable surviving Anglo-Saxon textiles are, however, the embroidered stole and maniple of St Cuthbert [Pl. 68]. These brilliant objects were woven and embroidered at Winchester between 909 and 916 and presented, twenty years later, to the shrine of St Cuthbert by King Æthelstan. The blending on these objects of gold, brilliant colours and pastel shades demonstrates the genius of English embroidery, which in later centuries was to become justly admired throughout Europe.

Although jewellery is rarely seen in Anglo-Saxon manuscript illustrations, it is obvious from the large number of brooches and other jewellery found in the graves of the pagan period that the Anglo-Saxons delighted in decking themselves with knick-knacks. No other subject in Anglo-Saxon archaeology has received so much attention as the brooches; they are a typologist's dream. It is often forgotten, however, that brooches were integral parts of everyday dress in the days before buttons. Basically there were three types of Anglo-Saxon brooch, the ring (or penannular) brooch, the bow brooch and the disc brooch. The ring brooches and penannular brooches are derived from pre-Roman Celtic forms and, until the seventh and eighth centuries, are often rather plain, apart from occasional more exotic examples. In the Northumbrian, Pictish and Irish areas, in the eighth and ninth centuries, penannular and pseudo-penannular brooches with large expanded terminals were developed. The terminals were decorated with animal ornaments in the style of the period. Another type was evolved with spherical, brambled terminals.

More commonly found are the various types of bronze bow brooch, which developed from the Iron Age and Roman safety-

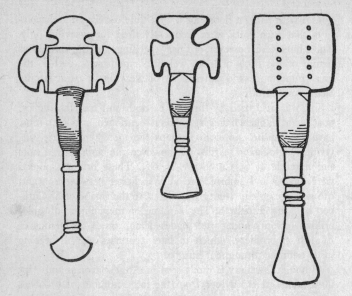

Fig. 19. Small long-brooches from Stapenhill, Staffs, Rothwell, Northants, and Icklingham, Suffolk

pin type of brooch, under a certain amount of Eastern European influence. These take many forms, some simple and others more elaborate. The great square-headed brooches (some of which are made of silver) and the cruciform brooches [Pl. 20] are often as much as 15 cm. in length, while some of the so-called 'small-long' brooches [Fig. 19] are barely 6 cm. in length. The square-headed brooches are often decorated with chip-carved ornament; cruciform brooches are often plainer in form. The brooch, with the main ornamental elements, was cast and then touched up with chisel and punch. The catch plate and hinge lugs, which carried the spring-pin, were then brazed on the back, while the face of the brooch, if it were a particularly grand example, was gilded. This type of brooch died out towards the end of the sixth century.

The third type of brooch, which is of circular form, has Roman

2

3

4

5

6

7

8

9

10

11

13

14

15

17

18

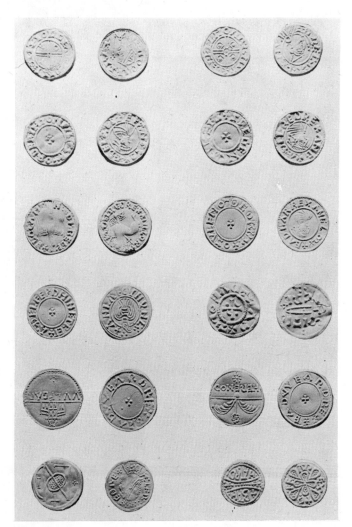

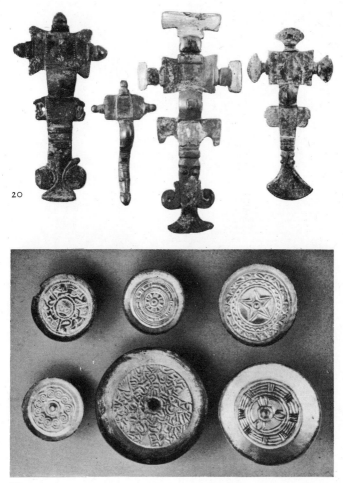

20

21

22 23

24 25

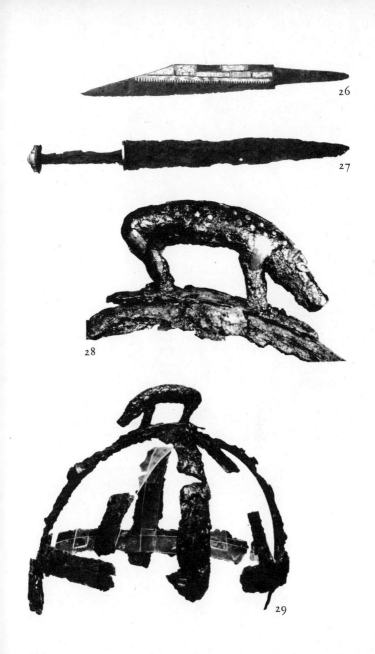

26

27

28

29

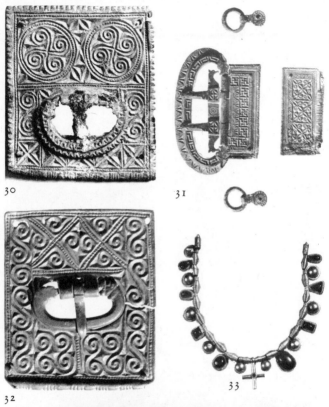

30　　　　　　　　　31

32　　　　　　　　　33

34

39

40

41

42

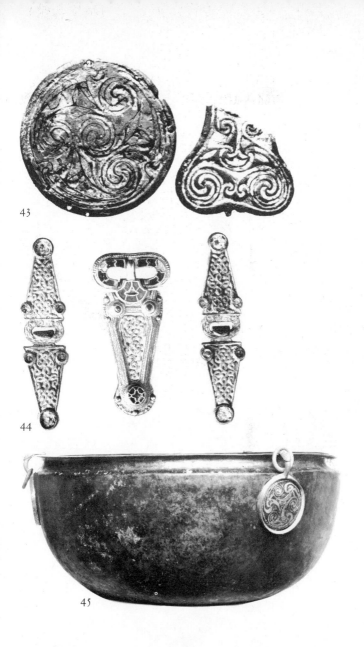

43

44

45

47

48

49

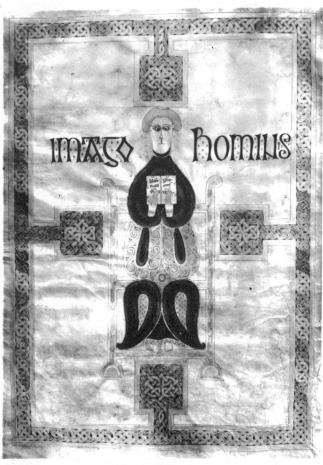

imago homiıs

53

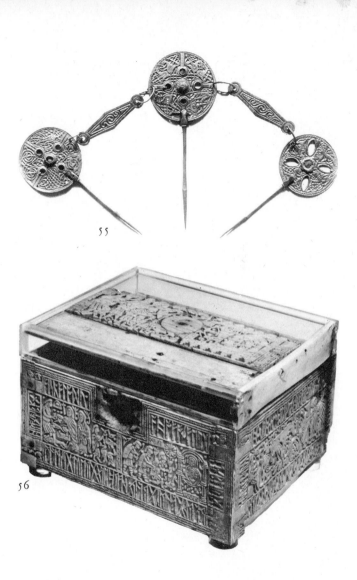

55

56

57   58

59

60

61

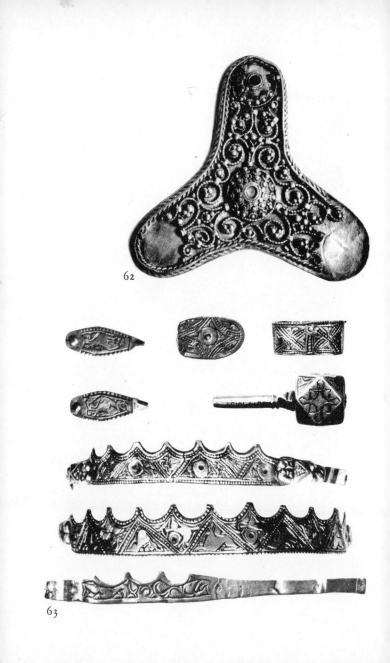

62

63

64

65

66

67

69

70

73

74

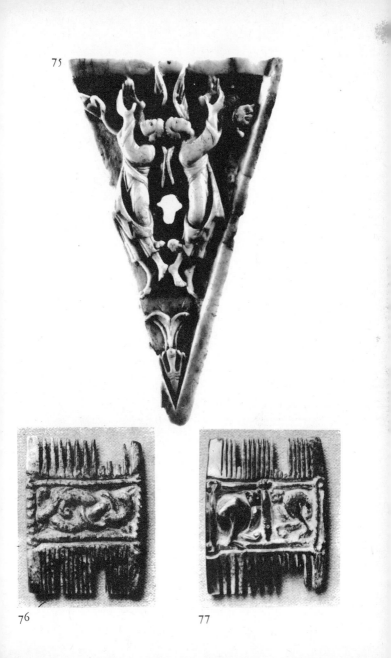

75

76 77

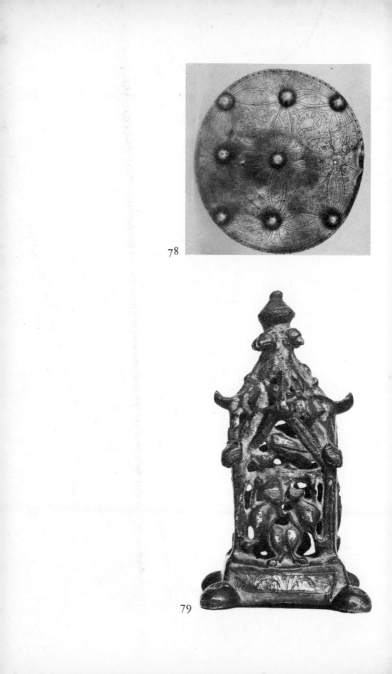

78

79

precursors. There are many forms of circular brooch: some are merely plain bronze discs decorated with ring and dot or other mechanical ornament, while others have a silvered or tinned surface. More elaborate are the cast and gilded saucer brooches [Pl. 21], which have a Rhenish ancestry. The richest disc brooches are, of course, the great polychrome jewels of Kent [Pls. 35–8], which are discussed at some length below (p. 136f.). In the Christian period disc brooches are found which are sometimes very elaborate objects of silver and gold. They are usually dished like a watch glass, and the largest is about 13 cm. in diameter.

Brooches of other forms naturally occur; small brooches in the shape of birds and animals were adopted by the pagan Anglo-Saxons from Continental models, while in the Christian period brooches in the shape of a cross are not unknown.

The smaller brooches (saucer brooches, small-long brooches, etc.) are usually found, in pairs, in women's graves of the fifth and sixth century; they were apparently worn on either side of the tunic above the bosom and, occasionally, festoons of beads were suspended between them. In the seventh century, as we have seen, brooches are usually found singly and were probably used to fasten the cloak, or mantle, at the shoulder. This method of fastening the cloak can be seen illustrated in various manuscripts and sculptures. Apparently these larger brooches were worn by both men and women.

Necklaces of glass beads, amber and even, occasionally, beautifully shaped amethyst drops are quite common in Anglo-Saxon graves. They are never illustrated in manuscripts but, from their position in the graves of the pagan dead, it seems that they were usually worn as festoons either pinned or sewn to the garment above the breast. Now and again more splendid necklaces of gold or garnet are found, as, for example, at Desborough in Northamptonshire [Pl. 33], where a series of gold pendants and gold-mounted cabochon garnets, with an equal-armed cross in the centre, is spaced by a series of barrel-shaped gold beads.

In the pagan period and probably later a chatelaine with imitation keys – T-shaped pieces of flat bronze, known as girdle hangers – and possibly a double-sided bone comb would hang at a woman's waist. She would occasionally wear ear-rings of bronze or silver and even a finger-ring. The braided cuff of her tunic might be fastened, if she lived in East Anglia, with a pair of plates of a rather elaborate hook-and-eye form and, if she were wealthy, she might have jewelled ends to her girdle. Bangles of silver, bronze or glass might be worn on her arm, and even on her leg; in the seventh century a small bronze drum-like needle-case might also hang at her waist. A fairly wealthy farmer's wife might wear a great deal of jewellery and would probably look most colourful. Her husband's sword belt, which hung over his right shoulder, might have a large ornamented buckle, but if he were too poor to own a sword he might have a buckled belt at his waist, attached to which would almost certainly be a sheath bearing a small wooden-hilted knife.

POTTERY

As in most periods of man's history pottery is one of the most important material survivals of the Anglo-Saxon period. In the pagan period the wheel-turned, highly industrialized, pottery of the Romans gave way – in most places – to hand-made vessels, some of which are of very poor quality. Traces of the kilns of these pagan Anglo-Saxon potters are rare, but at Cassington in Oxfordshire the remains of a very simple kiln have been excavated. The best preserved consisted of a hollow stoke-hole, about 90 cm. in diameter, connected by a 30 cm.-wide throat to a small oval firing chamber, about 38 cm. across. Traces of the heavily burnt limestone, which presumably lined and roofed the stoke-hole, were found together with burnt clay which bore marks of wattle. The stoke-pit had presumably been covered with a wattle and daub dome to form a simple up-draught kiln. Pottery fired in the two kilns has also been found: generally it consists of fairly rough bag-shaped jars of no particular quality or distinction. Another possible kiln excavated at Buckden, Hunts., may not have been used for pottery, but for corn drying. A pit which was interpreted by E. T. Leeds as a puddling pit for potter's clay, found at Sutton Courtenay, Berkshire, is the only other possible survivor of the pagan Anglo-Saxon potter's plant.

That pagan Anglo-Saxon pottery was occasionally manufactured on a commercial scale is demonstrated by the so called Illington/Lackford pottery [Fig. 20b] recognized by Dr Myres at cemeteries in west Norfolk, west Suffolk and Cambridgeshire – at Illington, Lackford, Rushford, West Stow Heath, Little Wilbrahan and the Cambridge cemetery on St John's College cricket field. This was a highly organized mid-sixth-century pottery, producing fairly stereotyped hand-raised pottery of good quality. The Illington/Lackford kilns, however, have not yet been found.

Excavation has, however, yielded a considerable body of evidence concerning the kilns of the middle and late Saxon period, kilns which have produced Ipswich, Thetford and Torksey ware (see below). The Thetford ware kilns have been described above (p. 83), and indicate a well-developed industry of surprising sophistication, producing the hard grey wheel-turned pottery so typical of this site which is found throughout eastern England between the ninth century and the Conquest. The evidence at Ipswich, while less clear, shows that there were many kilns in this town particularly in the Cox Lane area. Two kilns of the latest Saxon and earliest Norman period found at Torksey (producing pottery very similar to Thetford ware) reveal the central pedestal and (in one case) the fire-bars which support the floor of the kiln – we may see here the whole of the lower flue of an up-draught kiln.

In much of southern England in the late Anglo-Saxon period pottery was of an extremely coarse quality, often little better than that found in the pagan period. In Stamford in Lincolnshire, however, a more remarkable pottery is found. Like the Thetford and Torksey wares this pottery is made on a fast wheel. In fabric it has, however, a fine hard white quality which is sometimes embellished with pale green and yellow glazes. One kiln of probable Anglo-Saxon date has been excavated at Stamford. Unfortunately the stoke-hole was destroyed by Victorian builders, but the arched flue of the firing pit survived, linking it in form with the kilns at Torksey and Thetford. A large number of wasters were found in the body of the kiln, mostly fragments of cooking pots, costrels, skillets and spouted bowls, most of which were unglazed.

Let us very summarily examine the pottery of the Anglo-Saxon period. First of all there is the very coarse featureless pottery of the settlement sites, pottery used for cooking and food-storage. Such pottery is often grey or black in colour, hand-raised and undecorated, it is sometimes found in inhumation graves, as at Sleaford, Lincs. [Fig. 20c]. Not all the pottery found on settlement sites is, however, undecorated; some of it is highly ornamented, approaching in quality that which is frequently found as containers of ashes in the cremation graves [Fig. 20a]. It is hard to generalize about this pottery which (more than any other class of Anglo-Saxon antiquity) shows distinct and close connexions with the Continental homeland of the Anglo-Saxons, but in the space at my disposal I can only offer a basic classification of the main types of pagan Anglo-Saxon pottery.

Typical Anglo-Saxon pottery of the pagan period [Fig. 20] has a fabric which varies in colour between black and grey-brown. It is hand-made and the ware is so soft that a finger-nail easily bites into it. Much of the finer funerary ware is decorated with largish, oval bosses or impressed stamps and incised lines – very occasionally animals are drawn and stamped on the vessel, but such occurrences are rare and the design is usually purely ornamental. Certain decorative features of the funerary pottery have been interpreted as of ethnic significance, and successful attempts have been made to link similar types of pottery in England and in the Continental homeland of the Anglo-Saxons; but, in the light of the mixed nature of the Anglo-Saxon population at the time of the settlement, extreme caution is necessary in any consideration of the origins of the people who used this pottery in England. Basically speaking, the Anglian pottery in the Continental homeland is decorated with simple horizontal linear motifs round the neck, above a zone of vertical ornament sometimes interspaced with small bosses on the shoulder of the pot. The Saxon pottery is decorated with elongated bosses, sometimes of complicated form, below the shoulder of the pot, and vertical slashed or stamped ornament. The pottery of north-

centimetres

Fig. 20. Anglo-Saxon pottery of the pagan period: (a) biconical pot
with everted rim from Sancton, Yorks.; (b) globular urn made by the
Illington/Lackford potter from Lackford, Suffolk; (c) accessory vessel
from a grave at Sleaford, Lincs.; (d) *Buckelurne* from Hough-on-
the-Hill, Lincs.

western Europe and England reflects the community of the
area, but it is difficult to sort out in detail the different relationships within that community.

In a detailed lifelong study of the pottery of the Anglo-Saxon
period Dr Myres has reached certain general conclusions with
regard to the decoration of the pottery of the pagan period. The

earliest ornament consists of a vigorous linear decoration [Fig. 20a], emphasized occasionally by finger-tipping or dots. Occasionally there is a raised collar, which is often slashed. Late in the fifth century there is a tendency to use bold bosses which are pushed up from the interior of the pot; sometimes these bosses take strange and complicated forms (such pots, Fig. 20d, are known by their German name – *Buckelurnen*). During the sixth century the bosses become less elaborate, occurring only on the shoulder, and an increasing use of stamps is observed forming a background to the lines and bosses [Fig. 20b]. The stamped ornament becomes more elaborate during the second half of the sixth century and breaks up into meaningless and random embellishment in the seventh century. The form of the vessels can be classed in a number of groups of which five are decorated : (1) a bi-conical urn [Fig. 20a] usually of fifth-century date, (2) a hollow-necked variety of the same form which is also of early date, (3) a vessel of the same basic form as no (1) [Fig. 20b] but with a more rounded contour, dating from the late fifth until the end of the sixth century, (4) shouldered pots, dated around 500, (5) bowls, which fall early in the series. To these should be added various undecorated vessels of differing forms [Fig. 20c].

A different type of pottery is found in Kentish graves [Fig. 21a] : flask-shaped, it is usually red to buff in colour. Its form is probably based on that of Roman wine bottles and it may well have been made abroad in the Rhenish area and be the sole surviving fossil of the Continental wine trade of this early period. Coarse pottery of the normal Anglo-Saxon type rarely occurs in Kent.

Pottery of the type found at Sleaford is found in cemeteries and on pagan settlement sites all over England and occurs in such late seventh- and early eighth-century contexts as at the monastery of Whitby; while pottery of a similar form, though turned on a slow wheel, is found in eighth- and ninth-century contexts in East Anglia and elsewhere, as, for example, on the site of the Savoy palace in London. Our knowledge of this later pottery is drawn mainly from East Anglia. The kilns at Ipswich have already been discussed (p. 99). The ware produced there [Fig. 21b] is hard, sandy and greyish-black in colour. The

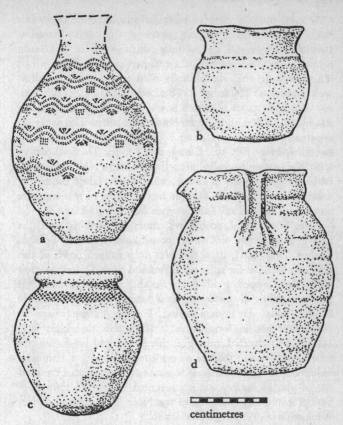

centimetres

Fig. 21. Wheel-turned Anglo-Saxon pottery: (a) Kentish bottle from grave 4, Holborough, Kent; (b) Ipswich ware jar without provenance (Ipswich Museum); (c) Thetford ware jar from Thetford; (d) spouted pitcher of Stamford ware from the site of St Leonard's priory, Stamford

pots have thick walls and sagging base and are occasionally decorated with a stamped ornament. Three forms are found: the simple cooking-pot, which is directly descended from the vessel of the pagan period found at Sleaford and elsewhere, a spouted pitcher and a bottle.

At some stage in the Middle Saxon period the use of the fast potter's wheel was introduced. Some of the pottery found at Ipswich, for example, demonstrates this fact. In the late Saxon period a far more accomplished pottery is found, known as Thetford ware after the Norfolk town where it was found in such profusion. The kilns at Thetford (p. 83) produced a variety of shapes: pitchers, angled bowls, large storage jars (some as much as three feet high), water-bottles and lamps. The pottery is apparently influenced by Rhenish prototypes, such as the *relief-band amphora* [Fig. 15]. Closely allied to the Thetford pottery is St Neots ware (so called after the town in Huntingdonshire) which is grey-purple in colour, with a soft fabric containing much crushed sea-shell. The commonest types of this ware are bowls with flanged rims and various forms of cooking-pot.

From Stamford, Lincolnshire, comes (as we have seen) the first glazed pottery known in post-Roman England. Spouted pitchers [Fig. 21d], jugs, jars and deep flanged bowls of this ware are found as far apart as Oxford and York. One of the most distinctive features of this pottery is that it is glazed in a light green or yellowish shade – the first glazed pottery to be seen in England since the Roman period. It is not known where the practice of glazing originated. It is possible that kilns were operating in Dutch Limburg at this period and producing this type of pottery, but there is no evidence of priority of dating on either side of the Channel. It is reasonably certain that the practice of glazing pottery was not invented in Western Europe: it was probably introduced from the Near East – glazed pottery is known from Persia and Byzantium.

While we have some knowledge of the pottery of East Anglia and the neighbouring counties in the later Anglo-Saxon period it should be emphasized that there were centres of production elsewhere in England, for example in Kent and at York and Chester. In the south and west of England a grass-tempered ware was produced, the use of which extended well into the post-Conquest period. Imported pottery was also used and is frequently found in the coastal towns of southern England.

GLASS

One of the most important groups of material found in Anglo-Saxon graves is the series of glass vessels which add a touch of lightness to the generally ponderous aspect of Anglo-Saxon antiquities. The forms produced by the Anglo-Saxon glass-blower, and his opposite number on the Continent, may have been stereotyped and the colours may not have been as rich as those used by the Romans but, compared with vessels of other material found in the Anglo-Saxon period, the variety of form and the attractive colours (yellows, greens, browns and blues) are extremely refreshing [Fig. 22].

Anglo-Saxon glass has been the special study of Dr Harden, and his work must form the basis of any summary of the subject. A fairly large number of Roman glasses (nearly thirty) has been found in Anglo-Saxon graves; particularly noticeable are the cone beakers such as that from Kempston in Bedfordshire [Fig. 22f.]. Glass of Anglo-Saxon type, made both in Britain and on the Continent, is found in some profusion. The commonest forms are the squat jars and the palm cups; less common are the bag beakers, and only two examples are known from this country of glass drinking-horns (both from Rainham, Essex). These rarer types, as well as the slightly more common, but hideous, claw-beakers, were almost certainly manufactured on the Continent and imported into this country by the wealthy. It is a noticeable feature that many of the glass vessels found in graves of the pagan period will not stand upright – a feature which can be observed in the later manuscripts, and in the Bayeux tapestry, where glasses are seen to lie and not stand on the table.

No glass kilns of the pagan Anglo-Saxon period are known to survive, but certain glasses, as, for example, the palm cup, are found in such quantities that they were very probably made in this country and it has been suggested that a glass house was situated somewhere in the neighbourhood of the richest of all Anglo-Saxon cemeteries, that at Faversham in Kent. The only glass kilns known in England were found recently at Glastonbury, Somerset. Under the north-east corner of the later medieval

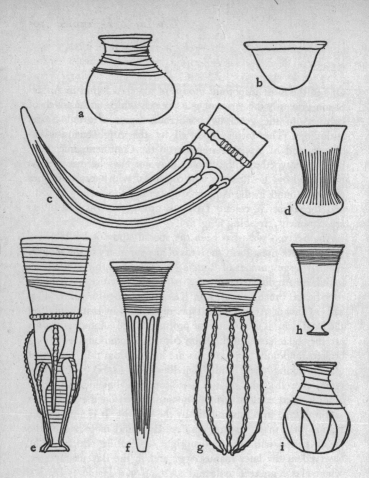

Fig. 22. Anglo-Saxon glassware: (a) squat jar, Upchurch, Kent; (b) palm cup, Faversham, Kent; (c) drinking-horn, Rainham, Essex; (d) bell beaker, Ashford, Kent; (e) claw-beaker, Taplow, Bucks.; (f) cone beaker, Kempston, Beds.; (g) bag beaker, Faversham, Kent; (h) stemmed beaker, Croydon, Surrey; (i) pouch bottle, Sare, Kent.

cloister were found the remains of the floors of three kilns. Fragments of glass, found in association with them, indicate a date in the ninth or tenth centuries. One of the kilns produced very few fragments of glass and it may be possible to interpret it as an annealing kiln. We must await the publication of these kilns, but we seem to have here the remains of the only known Anglo-Saxon glass factory in this country. We must presume, on the analogy of later glass houses, that all the kilns were under the same roof and that the glass-blowers, using tools not very different from those used today, produced their glass vessels in the area between the kilns.

CHAPTER FOUR

Weapons and Warfare

THIS was a heroic age: the vernacular literature makes this abundantly clear. Even Christ is seen as a heroic prince:

> Then the young hero, God Almighty,
> Firm and unflinching, stripped himself.

The greatest virtue was loyalty to one's lord: the warrior shared the spoils of battle, but he was also willing to die for his lord – indeed it was considered a disgrace to leave the field of battle if one's chief were dead. This spirit is reflected in both the poetry and prose of the Anglo-Saxons long after Christianity had become firmly established in England. War has left its remains in the archaeological record, in the form of innumerable weapons buried in the graves of warriors and peasants. It is fitting that when we deal with a heroic age we should consider these remains at some length.

Although the sword was the most important Anglo-Saxon weapon, it is not found with the frequency of other weapons in the graves of the male Anglo-Saxon. Baldwin-Brown, a long time ago, quoted some figures to demonstrate the comparative rarity of swords: two were found in the 308 graves from Kingston, seven came from the 150 graves at Bifrons, although at Sarre there was one sword in every ten graves. To these figures may be added some more modern results: one sword was found in the hundred graves excavated at Holywell Row and none at all in the 123 graves found at Burwell. We know from the documents of the Christian Saxon period that swords were precious objects, handed down from father to son. A sword which had belonged to Offa was bequeathed by an eleventh-century prince to his brother. Again and again we meet references in Anglo-Saxon poetry to swords which have greater virtue because they were old, or because they had belonged to some famous person of the past.

The sword was the weapon of the man of wealth and position. Some swords, as for example Beowulf's sword, *Naegling*, even bore names of their own. Few of these rich swords survive; at best, all that remains is a few mounts of bronze, or of more precious metal, which embellished the hilt [Pl. 2]. Now and again an exceptionally rich sword occurs to give us an impression of the wealth and position of its owner.

The earliest Anglo-Saxon swords, those of the pagan period, are two-edged and about 75 cm. long; they are thin-bladed with straight edges and rather rounded points. Known technically as a *spatha*, the Anglo-Saxon sword of the pagan period has a long and continuous ancestry that stems back to the Celtic La Tène sword, which is of similar length and shape. The sword was carried in a scabbard, which was usually made of two thin laths of leather-covered wood. The mouth of the scabbard was sometimes ornamented with a metal band; one of the most impressive examples, from Chessel Down, has a gilt-bronze ornamented pattern on one face and a runic inscription on the back. Some scabbards were bound with a strip of metal and were tipped with a metal chape, which occasionally, as at Brighthampton, was ornamented. The scabbard was sometimes lined with fleece, and this has been explained by the fact that the natural greases of the sheep's wool would keep the blade from rusting. Professor Atkinson was able to undertake a thorough examination of the scabbard of a sword from Petersfinger. It was made up of alternate layers of wood and leather, a thin wooden sheet on the inside, wood on one outer face and leather on the other, all bound round the edges with bronze. At Brushfield in Derbyshire, Thomas Bateman found a scabbard which was covered with leather ornamented with a series of lozenges, while a fragment of a similar scabbard [Pl. 25] was found at Hexham in Northumbria. The blade of the sword was comparatively thin and was occasionally decorated with a stamped design; two boards, for instance, appear on the blade of a sword from the

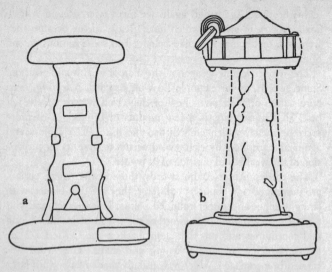

Fig. 23. Schematized drawings of sword hilts: (a) Cumberland (seventh century); (b) Gilton, Kent (sixth century); (c) no provenance (Viking); (d) Abingdon (ninth century – see pl. 22)

River Lark. Some blades are 'pattern welded'. This method of twisting bands of iron together and beating the resulting plait into a thin blade which is then edged with hard steel adds flexibility to a weapon. The face of the sword is then polished and the marbled effect achieved must be responsible for such passages as the description in *Beowulf*: 'Upon him gleams the ancient heirloom, the hard, ring-patterned sword, treasure of the Heathobards.' Often, however, the blade is beaten out of one piece of metal and is unornamented.

The hilt [Fig. 23] has been used to form the basis of a typological distinction between the various swords, but as yet no really satisfactory typology has been evolved. The hilt is built up round the tang which is a continuation of the blade. The guard, or quillions, consists usually of a simple insubstantial rectangular block of bone or wood, protecting 2·5 cm. on either side of the blade. The grip is of wood (less frequently of bone)

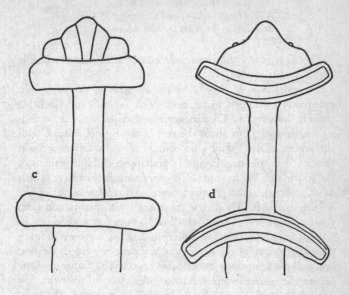

c   d

and is bound with cloth or leather, or even with silver wire or cord. Occasionally, as on a sword from Chessel Down, the grip is decorated with ornamental metal plates. The tang is riveted over a plate at the top of the hilt, and, to cover the rather rudimentary result, a pommel is often added which can be highly decorative. This pommel can take many forms; a sword found in a grave in the Fleam Dike, in Cambridgeshire, for example, has a spherical pommel; sometimes it is merely a very flat triangle of iron, but more often it has a sub-triangular shape, which has long rejoiced in the picturesque description of 'the cocked-hat pommel'. Some cocked-hat pommels are decorated with small rings, a few of which are free-running rings, while others are immovable and merely decorative. This feature, which in England is rare and largely confined to Kent, is a universal trait throughout Northern Europe and one is reminded of the passage in the Old Norse *Poetic Edda*:

> I know of swords lying in Sigarsholm . . .
> One among them the finest of all . . .
> A ring on the hilt, valour midway
> and fear on the point for him who wins it.

The ring, as has often been pointed out, is associated with the heroic quality of courage.

The early type of sword, the *spatha*, with its miserable hilt, apparently continued to be made well on into the Christian period; drawings in Carolingian manuscripts show us swords of similar form. But about the end of the eighth century, with the advent of the Vikings, an entirely revolutionary sword was developed in Western Europe – perhaps in Britain, perhaps in the Rhineland. We have in this country some fifty or sixty swords of this period, some of which were obviously weapons of the Viking invaders. They vary considerably in quality and size; most of them have blades which are between 75 and 80 cm. in length, have broad shallow fullers (a fuller is a groove running down the centre of the blade) and are pattern welded; the best are well-made, springy and double-edged. The rather pathetic hilt of the *spatha* is replaced by a more splendid one with fine projecting quillions, which may be straight or curved. The pommels can be divided roughly into two typological groups, one having a lobed shape and the other a flattened semicircular, or pointed ovoid cap; a few types fall into neither category.

The blades of these later swords are much stronger and heavier than those of the *spatha*. Occasionally welded into the blade is the name of the swordsmith who made them, some of which demonstrate that the sword was made abroad.

Some Anglo-Saxon hilts are very grand; for instance, the parcel-gilt silver pommel [Pl. 24] from Fetter Lane in the City of London, decorated with whirling snakes interspaced with a leaf pattern, is one of the most beautiful and accurately executed pieces of metalwork to have survived from this period. Slightly less grand is a sword from Abingdon, Berkshire [Pl. 22], which has silver plates inlaid into both the quillions and the pommel. The silver plates are decorated with animal, plant and even human motifs engraved and set with niello. There are parallels to the Abingdon sword from, for example, the River Witham, near Lincoln [Pl. 23], and from Dolven, Gronneberg and Hoven in Norway. The quillions and pommel are usually of iron, over-laid occasionally with silver but often merely decorated with a punched ornament; sometimes however they are of bronze, as, for example, the pommel-guard from Exeter which bears the name of the maker in the Latin inscription EOFRI MEFE (*Eofri me fecit*, Eofri made me). As most of the swords of this period found in England are casual finds, we know less about the scabbard than we do for the earlier period. However, traces of wood and rather elaborate chapes and mounts from scabbard openings indicate that they were little different from their pagan forerunners. The sword hung at the left hip, being carried in a baldric which passed over the right shoulder [Fig. 24].

Related to the sword is the single-edged long-knife – the *scramasax*. Such knives were used by the men who murdered Sigibert in 575. Gregory of Tours described them as 'strong knives, commonly called *scramasaxes*, smeared with poison'. This statement has presumably been responsible for the un-doubtedly false assumption that the grooving on the blades of the *scramasaxes* held poison. The term '*scramasax*' covers a multitude of knives from the very short knife, no more than 7.5 cm. long, to the considerable weapon which may be as much as 75 cm. in length. Here we shall concentrate on the weapons only.

The typical *scramasax* [Pls. 26, 27] of the Migration period, as found on the Continent, is a clumsy object about 40 cm. in length with an asymmetrical tang, though occasionally, as at Pouan, the weapon is as much as 52 cm. in length and has a beautifully decorated hilt. *Scramasaxes* do not appear in this country until the latter part of the pagan period and their variety of shapes makes it difficult to generalize concerning them – for instance, one of the *scramasaxes* found at Uncleby in Yorkshire is 60 cm. in length, while others may be as little as 35 cm. long. They were carried in a sheath at a man's thigh and the sheath was suspended from the belt by means of a series of small bronze loops. The guard of the *scramasax* is often very insignificant, while the pommel can vary considerably in shape, from an unobtrusive 'cocked-hat' to the more elaborate silver pommel of the Winchester *scramasax* [Pl. 27]; this is tripartite with a central lobe flanked by two shoulders which, in their design, are reminiscent of animal heads. An important, though later, *scramasax* pommel comes from Windsor, the central lobe of which is inlaid with a gold panel covered with interlaced filigree wire ornament, the thicker wire terminating in exquisite

Fig. 24. Warrior portrayed in late Saxon manuscript (British Museum, Cotton Tiberius, C.VI)

animal heads, while bunches of grapes made of small granules of gold enrich the design even further.

The tradition of the pagan *scramasax* continues through into the Christian Saxon period: the *scramasaxes* from Ofton and Hoxne in Suffolk and from the Thames at Wandsworth may well belong to the eighth century. But the true late Saxon *scramasaxes* are typified by two fine examples in the British Museum, one from the Thames and the other from Sittingbourne in Kent [Pl. 26]. The Thames *scramasax* is 71 cm. long and has an inlaid mosaic along its upper edge made up of copper, bronze and silver wire in triangles and lozenges. Also inlaid is the whole of the *futhorc*, or runic alphabet. The Sittingbourne *scramasax* is ornamented with inlaid panels decorated with an early expression of the Winchester art style of the early tenth century; it carries the name of both its owner and its maker, Sigebereht and Biorktelm. Many other *scramasaxes* of this later group are inlaid with copper or bronze wire and in fact the technique continues into the thirteenth century. It would be best to think of these *scramasaxes* as daggers, although many of the later, larger weapons may well have been more useful as a sword.

The commonest weapon of defence, of which traces are found in Anglo-Saxon graves, is the shield [Fig. 25]. The Anglo-Saxon shield comprises a round wooden board, known as an orb, with an iron boss in the centre. The orb is sometimes covered with leather and a central hole allows the knuckles of the hand to manoeuvre within the hollow formed by the boss, the grip being attached at this place. Some of the shields were bound at the rim with a metal binding, but this is rare and a leather binding was presumably more common. The shields vary in size. The smallest shield recorded in England is one of 30 cm. in diameter found at Petersfinger, Wiltshire, and the largest, 76 cm. in diameter, came from Ringmer, Sussex. Traces of the orb are rarely found in Anglo-Saxon graves and these figures must be treated with caution. At Caenby, Lincolnshire, however, part of the orb of a substantial shield survived; it must have been at least 3 cm. thick and was decorated with a series of gilt-bronze plaques decorated with interlace ornament. Judging by the few examples where the handle and the boss have been riveted together through the orb and where the wood has survived, it would appear that pagan Anglo-Saxon shields were often not much more than 12 mm. in thickness – in fact, not unlike the surviving Viking shields found in the Gokstad vessel in Norway which have a large and surprisingly thin orb. Such a shield would be light and easily handled in battle.

The orbs were usually made of lime wood and were sometimes covered with leather, as at Sutton Hoo; the orbs of some shields would be painted, as in the Viking Gokstad find. All the surviving shield bosses are made of iron and are of three main shapes, one with concave sides and a carination, one with convex sides, and one conical. They are riveted to the orb through the flange, sometimes with bronze or gilt-headed rivets. They are usually beaten out of a single piece of metal, but occasionally, as in the Melbourn cemetery, a conical shield boss was made by bending a flat sheet of metal to form a cone. The boss is often

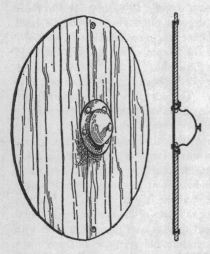

Fig. 25. Reconstructed Anglo-Saxon shield (after Wheeler)

tipped with a button which can sometimes be elaborately decorated with a silver or bronze plaque.

There has been considerable discussion as to whether the shields were curved like a watch glass. It has been said more than once that 'the angle of the boss flange indicates a considerable curvature to the surface of the shield'. Such an argument may well be false. The angle of the flange of the boss is probably an accident of manufacture, as it would be considerably more difficult to produce a boss with a flat flange, as distinct from an angled flange, because of the stresses in the metal. At the same time an angled flange would provide a better grip on the wood when the rivets were fastened. So very few complete shields have survived that the evidence is not conclusive. In the whole of Northern Europe, however, not a single curved shield orb has been found. There is some evidence that the orb of the Sutton Hoo shield was curved, the long attachments of the grip apparently providing for a curved board; similar evidence has been put forward in favour of curved shields in Italy and Germany. Detailed examination of the grip of one of the shields from Petersfinger, Wilts., has convinced the excavators that the shield was curved, with a radius of curvature of about 50 cm. The structure of this shield is of great interest, Professor Atkinson having shown that the shield orb was 'built up of two or more

Fig. 26. Shields, spearheads and battle-axes, illustrated in Anglo-Saxon manuscripts

thicknesses of wood with the grain of one lamination running at right angles to the next, as in modern plywood'. He suggests that this structure was necessary in building up a convex shield, and that the orb was made up of a number of narrow strips laid side by side. The nineteenth-century description of the find of a shield at Linton may perhaps be illuminated in the light of the Petersfinger example: 'Enough was preserved to show the form to have been circular, and laths of wood converged from the extremity to the umbo. These laths were fastened to the body of the shield, probably of wood, with twine.' The precise meaning of this description is obscure, but it has a remarkable coincidence with the description of the Petersfinger shield and it is possible that these shields were conical or curved. There can be little doubt therefore that curved shields were used by the Saxons and this is confirmed by manuscript illustrations [Fig. 26].

The shield and the spear were the common arms of the average soldier, and it is probable that some shields were made of wood and leather alone and that only the richer members of the community had shields with an iron boss. At Oberflacht in Germany, for example, an oval wooden shield covered with leather and without a boss was discovered. Tacitus, writing of the Germanic peoples at the beginning of our era, describes shields of wickerwork. It is not impossible that the Anglo-Saxons occasionally copied this form of construction. Most of the Anglo-Saxon shields illustrated in the contemporary manuscripts are round, while most of the shields illustrated in the Bayeux tapestry are kite-shaped. We have, however, no other evidence of a kite-shaped shield at this early date. One thing that emerges from the manuscript and tapestry evidence is that the shield of the late Saxon period was already being used for some sort of heraldic display. We cannot be sure that the signs on the shields indicated anything more than sympathetic magic or personal artistic taste, but it seems probable that certain signs indicated a clan or a sept.

'*Arma, id est scutum et lancum*' (a man's arms are the shield and the spear) say the Frankish laws, and the ordinary Saxon must have fought mainly with these two weapons. Iron spearheads are the commonest weapon found in Anglo-Saxon contexts, yet, probably because they are so uninterestingly uniform, these have never been studied with the thoroughness accorded to other weapons. But the spear, not only a weapon of war but an implement of the hunt, is found both in the poor man's grave and, as at Sutton Hoo, in the grave of the king. The weapon of Woden was used universally and some of the finer spearheads decorated with inlaid precious metal indicate something of the value of this weapon in the mind of the Anglo-Saxon.

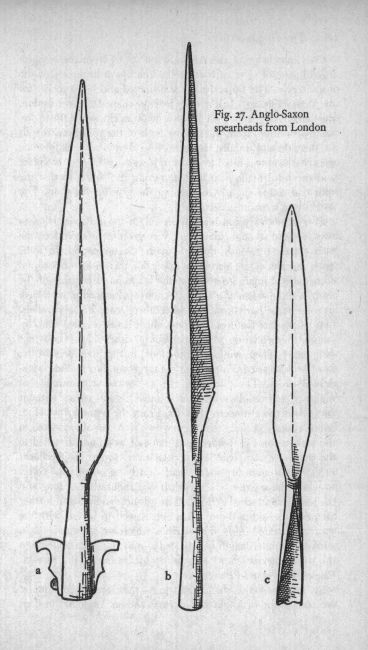

Fig. 27. Anglo-Saxon spearheads from London

a   b   c

Our knowledge of the Anglo-Saxon spear, from the archaeological point of view, is based on the iron tips or heads and on the
iron ferrule. The tip is usually leaf-shaped and has a socket for
the shaft [Fig. 27]. It is usually lozenge-shaped in cross section,
the blade rising from the edge to a medium rib, while the socket
which continues from the narrow neck of the spearhead is split
on the side and usually carries an iron rivet. Presumably when
the spearhead was fitted to its shaft, it was first riveted into place
and the head made firm by hammering the socket so that the
split end closed slightly, tightening the grip on the shaft. The
socket was sometimes decorated.

Spearheads vary considerably in length from a few inches to
two feet and, though some have very prominent shoulders, the
form varies very little throughout the Saxon period. In some
cases the blades are pattern welded but this is an uncommon
occurrence. Lunate grooving of the blade on either side of the
midrib, often taken as a sign of Saxon workmanship, may have
its roots in the Early Iron Age, where there are technical parallels.
One of the late features, and one which is often called Carolingian, is the two wings which stick out on either side of the socket
[Fig. 27a]. These wings are functional in that they prevent the
head of the spear from piercing the target too far, making withdrawal easier. These features can be noticed in a number of
manuscripts from the ninth century onwards and are not without
parallel in more modern contexts. From the manuscripts [Fig.
26] it appears possible that these wings were not always fixed to
the socket; some may have been made of wood and attached to
the shaft. No complete Saxon spear survives; but at Oberflacht
in Germany an entire spear was found lying outside the coffin
in which the warrior was buried. It was about 210 cm. long and
the head was attached to the shaft by gilt-headed nails and further
bound by a leather thong. This agrees well in length with the
spears illustrated in the manuscripts, which are often taller than
a man. A similar length is indicated also by the distance between
the tip of the spearhead and the tip of the ferrule in graves at
Chessel Down and Petersfinger.

Sword, *scramasax*, shield and spear – these are the commonest
weapons found in Anglo-Saxon graves and on Anglo-Saxon sites.

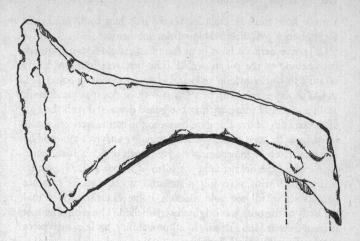

Fig. 28. *Francisca*, or throwing axe, from Howletts, Kent. London, British Museum

We must, however, deal with certain other armour which is found more rarely: the axe, the helmet, the bow and arrow, the angon and the coat of mail. A popular weapon of the pagan period on the Continent was the *francisca* or throwing axe [Fig. 28], which has a comparatively short handle and a head which curves upwards from the handle at a wide angle to a slightly upturned blade. This form is mainly Frankish but, although of rare occurrence, it is found in this country, mainly in Kent; one example, from Howletts, has an inlaid gilt plate on the head. A commoner type of axe in the later Saxon period is that which has a blade with a broad curved edge, mounted at right angles to the shaft [Fig. 26]; this was used as a battle-axe in hand-to-hand fighting and it is seen put to this use in the Bayeux tapestry, by which time the battle-axe is a particularly English weapon (Stenton describes it as the traditional weapon of the house-carles) although it had not ousted the spear. This type of axe, with the curved and often drooping blade, was probably also used for chopping wood (although the T-shaped axe was particularly used for this purpose). Such axes as that from Sutton Hoo, which has a metal haft, must be a battle-axe; the iron haft could not be cut through by a well-directed blow from another axe.

Only two helmets have been found in Anglo-Saxon contexts; both belong to the pagan period. The first was found at Benty Grange in Derbyshire in 1848 and is a very elaborate object [Pl. 29]. The cap is made up of a framework of flat iron bands built up in a spherical form, with a nose guard decorated with the sign of the cross in silver. The gaps between the bands were originally filled in with horn plates (which no longer survive) attached by means of rivets with ornamental silver heads of double-axe shape. The crest of the helmet is in the form of a boar [Pl. 28], which is decorated with silver-gilt plates and studs, and its eyes are garnets set in filigree gold mounts. It has been suggested that the body of the boar was originally enamelled. The second helmet is from Sutton Hoo: this is, in all probability, an imported piece and has been discussed elsewhere.

The presence of the boar, a Celtic symbol of some importance, on the Benty Grange helmet illuminates a number of passages in Anglo-Saxon literature, particularly one from *Beowulf*, where a helmet is personified as a boar:

> On that pyre could be plainly seen
> the bloody mail shirt and the golden swine,
> The iron-hard boar ...

The 'golden ... iron-hard boar' must be related to the most conspicuous part of the Benty Grange helmet.

The helmet was not a common piece of armour in the Saxon period – it seems to have been worn only by a chieftain or a rich man. On the Franks Casket, for instance, only the helmets of the leaders are depicted with neck guards and nose pieces; other warriors have soft leather (?) hats. Even on the Continent, in the contemporary Germanic graves, helmets are rare, although they occur in France, Germany and Sweden much more frequently than in England. In the manuscripts of the Christian period the helmet appears to be worn chiefly by those in authority. The type of helmet worn by the warrior, with its conical cap and nose guard, was evidently in common use among the cavalry at the battle of Hastings. Unfortunately no helmets of this type survive in this country, although comparable examples exist elsewhere, for example the helmet of St Wenceslaus in Prague Cathedral, which like the Benty Grange helmet has a Christian symbol (in this case the Crucifixion) on the nose guard. It seems probable that by the end of the Saxon period the helmet was a common piece of armour, as witness the reference in the *Anglo-Saxon Chronicle* for 1008 where every eight hides of land had to provide a helmet and a corselet. But Miss Keller is doubtless right when she says that the helmet was a comparatively rare piece of armour until this period. The ordinary soldier probably wore the so-called Phrygian cap, which may have been, as Laking suggests, lined with metal.

Archers are represented on the eighth-century Franks Casket [Pl. 56], on the Bayeux tapestry and in numerous manuscripts of the Anglo-Saxon period. Bows and arrows are, however, extremely rare in Anglo-Saxon graves. At Chessel Down, Hillier records that 'the presence of the bow, about five feet in length, could be distinctly traced by the dark line of decomposed wood in the chalk', and Baldwin-Brown records a similar feature at Bifrons. Also at Chessel Down were found arrowheads and traces of the shafts of a number of arrows, which the excavator presumed were made of the 'small straight wood of the hazel'. Arrowheads are sometimes found, but they are not a common Anglo-Saxon antiquity and Baldwin-Brown has pointed out that they may easily be confused with the head of a spear or a javelin; there appear to be both socketed and tanged arrowheads, some of which were certainly barbed, but one must presume that most arrows had no metal point and were merely hardened in the fire. At Oberflacht in Swabia for example a series of arrows was found, each some 60 cm. in length, which were 'so withered that we took them for bowstrings'; no arrowheads were attached to them and only a brownish colouring was seen where the points should have been. At this same site were found a number of bows, one of which was about 2 m. long. They were made of yew and were thickest in the centre, tapering towards the end and slightly curved.

The bow was the weapon of the foot soldier and of the common man and served for both the chase and for battle. The arrows

Fig. 29. Transporting weapons, from the Bayeux Tapestry

were carried in a quiver, which was slung over the shoulder, and were flighted with feathers. The bows in the Bayeux tapestry appear to be about 1.2 m. in length but it would be unwise to make any judgement of size from contemporary illustration alone. A much longer one has been found at Hedeby in Germany, while the only surviving early medieval bow from England, that from Berkhamsted Castle which may be of an early thirteenth-century date, is about 1.2 m. in length. It has been suggested that the bow was not a typical Anglo-Saxon weapon; perhaps there is some truth in this in the light of Henry of Huntingdon's record of William the Conqueror's reproach of the Saxons for their bad bowmanship.

Agathias, writing of the wars between Justinian and the Teutonic invaders of Italy, records that the chief weapon of the invaders was a light, barbed weapon which could be used as a javelin or in hand-to-hand fighting. 'The haft is covered with lamina so that little wood can be seen.' Agathias's description is a little confusing, and attempts to identify the weapon described have never been entirely satisfactory. It may be the *angon*, which is mainly found on the Continent, but which does occur in this country and especially in Kent, where it has been found at Sarre, Bifrons, High Down and Strood. Another example comes from Beddington in Surrey. But these weapons are so undoubtedly foreign, and so rare of occurrence in the Anglo-Saxon area, that we need not discuss them here.

The coat of mail, which can be seen so frequently on the Bayeux tapestry, is a rare find in this country. Fragments of a mail-coat have been found at Sutton Hoo and the Benty Grange helmet was covered with mail when found. Nothing survives of the Benty Grange mail and it is possible that it was merely the neck guard of the helmet (a helmet with a mail neck guard occurred in the more or less contemporary grave 6 at Valsgärde in Sweden). The mail from the Sutton Hoo grave is corroded together, but undoubtedly formed a mail shirt. It differs from all the other surviving pre-Conquest chain-mail in Europe in that the links are not riveted, but merely butted together – a weak

Fig. 30. Warrior, from the Bayeux Tapestry

construction that had nothing to recommend it save ease of manufacture. The mail shirts depicted in the Bayeux tapestry [Figs. 29, 30] have short wide sleeves and skirts which are divided in front and behind, for ease in riding. Sir James Mann has pointed out that these splits in the skirt must not be interpreted as an indication that the shirt was a garment which looked like a pair of combinations; the discomforts of riding in such a garment would have taxed the endurance of even the hardiest Viking. Such suits of mail must have been expensive to make and were obviously worn only by leaders and chieftains, a leather jerkin being sufficient protection for the more humble members of society. The mail shirt would itself be worn over a leather jerkin or even over a padded vest, so that the interlocking rings might not be driven into the flesh when pierced.

In order to examine the method of warfare used by the Anglo-Saxons, I have taken a description of a battle and drawn from it conclusions as to the handling of weapons and the methods of fighting. On 11 August 991, near Maldon in Essex, was fought the battle which is known by the name of that town. It was fought on the banks of the River Blackwater; the Danes were initially on the Island of Northey and ultimately crossed, as a result of the Saxons' bad strategy, to the mainland by means of a causeway that is visible to this day. The battle was commemorated by a tapestry, which no longer exists, presented to the Abbey of Ely by the widow of Byrhtnoth, the English leader, and by the vernacular Anglo-Saxon poem which I have translated below. I have cut from the poem some of the rhetorical passages, which, though interesting, do not concern us here:

Then he ordered each soldier to dismount and drive his horse away from the field and to rely on his hand and his steadfastness. Then Byrhtnoth began to draw up his men; he rode and advised them, told them how they should stand and keep their ranks, and how they might best hold their shields firm with their hands. He encouraged them. When he had drawn up his army he dismounted among those people who pleased him most, where his retainers were most devoted. [At this point the Vikings send a messenger offering to refuse battle if the English will give them money; this offer is con-

temptuously turned down.] Then he [Byrhtnoth] ordered the warriors, carrying their shields, to move forward until they all stood on
the river bank. [After holding the causeway for a short time
Byrhtnoth over-confidently allows the enemy to cross the ford.]
Then the battle wolves, the Viking horde, were not hampered by the
water. They came over the Blackwater with their shields, westwards
over the gleaming flood, the seamen with their linden shields.
Byrhtnoth and his men stood there waiting for the enemy. He ordered
them to form a wall with their shields and to stand firm against the
foe. The fight, and the glory which comes with it, was now close at
hand. The time was now come when the doomed should fall. All was
clamour, ravens circled above, the eagle eager for carrion. There was
a cry on the earth.

They let the file-hardened spears, the grim-ground javelins, fly
from the hand. Bows were busy, point pierced shield, the rush of
battle was fierce, warriors fell on all sides, the young men lay dead.
. . . Byrhtnoth's kinsman, his sister's son, was cruelly hewn down by
swords. . . . A man hardened in battle advanced to meet the warrior
[i.e. Byrhtnoth] and raised his weapon, his shield as his defence. The
earl, in no way less bold, advanced towards the 'churl', each bent on
evil to the other. Then the Viking threw a southern spear, which
wounded the lord of the warriors, who banged the spear with his
shield so that the shaft broke; the spear was shivered and fell away
from him. The warrior was angry and with his spear struck the
proud Viking who had given him the wound. The warrior was
skilful and ran his spear through the young warrior's neck; his hand
guided it so that it killed the Viking.

Then he struck another raider so that his corselet burst and he was
wounded in the breast through the chain mail; the fatal point reached
his heart. [Byrhtnoth is again wounded.] A man then advanced on
the earl to rob him of his warrior's trappings, the spoil and rings and
ornamented sword.

Then Byrhtnoth drew his broad and brown-edged sword from his
sheath and struck him on his corselet. Too quickly another Viking
checked his hand, crippling the earl's arm. The yellow-hilted sword
fell to the ground and he could not hold or use a weapon. [After a
heroic speech Byrhtnoth and his two retainers were killed, whereupon
some warriors flee the field while others are rallied by heroic speeches
and are gradually struck down.] Then, eagerly, the hostage helped
them; he was called Ascferth and was the son of Ecglaf, and came
from a good Northumbrian family. He did not draw away from the
fight, but shot his arrows unceasingly, sometimes hitting a shield,

sometimes a warrior. As long as he could wield his weapons, he dealt out wounds as much as he could.

Edward the Tall stood yet at the forefront of the battle. . . . He broke the shield-wall and fought with the warriors until he had worthily taken vengeance on the seamen for the death of his chief and lay among the slain.

That noble retainer Ætheric, the brother of Sibirht, eager and impetuous, also fought boldly, as did many others; they hacked away the beaked shield and were valiant. The rim of the shield burst and the war-shirt sang a fearful song. . . . Then were the shields broken: the Vikings advanced enraged by the battle. . . . Byrhtwold, an old retainer, spoke, raised aloft his shield, shook his ashen-spear and encouraged the warriors boldly. 'Purpose shall be harder, heart more valiant, courage greater as strength grows weaker. Here lies our lord, cut down, the noble man in the dust. He who thinks to turn now from the fight will long regret it. I am old. I will not flee but will lie by the side of my lord – that so much loved man.'

This poem, written not long after the battle while individual acts of valour were still fresh in the mind, enables us to reconstruct something of the art of war in the Anglo-Saxon period.

As was usual in Anglo-Saxon times the battle was fought on foot. Anglo-Saxon battles were fairly solid affairs: once the forces had met, the battle consisted of grim hand-to-hand fighting in a restricted area, the opposing sides hacking away at each other until one side was reduced to carrion or broke and fled. It is obvious from this poem that, despite the well-organized political structure of the period, the army was bound by the pagan heroic tradition based on the warrior's duty to his lord: when the chief was in the ascendant his companion or retainer enjoyed the glory and the spoils of victory; conversely, the retainer suffered with his chief, even, like Byrhtwold and Ætheric, dying by their chief's side. It was considered something of a disgrace to flee from battle after the death of one's chief (although by the late Anglo-Saxon period even 'the right side' could flee with some impunity), and even a Christian like Asser cannot help letting a hint of criticism creep into his writings when the Saxons fled from the field after the death of a chief. As a consequence, battles were bloody and long drawn-out affairs.

From the Maldon poem it can be seen that the leader of the

Anglo-Saxons took some care to draw up his men in line of battle. He was apparently at pains to create a wall of shields. It has been suggested that this shield-wall was in the nature of the Roman *testudo*, that, to use Professor Gordon's words, 'the shield-wall was a defensive formation made by ranks of men placed closely one behind another and holding their shields side by side and overlapping so as to present a continuous wall. The front rank of men held their shields before their breasts and the ranks behind held theirs over their heads to protect both those in front and themselves.' This interpretation must be basically true (*pace* Oman), but there is a certain formality about it which seems foreign to the idea of a Saxon battle. First of all I think we must discount the idea that the shields were interlocked; this would give no room to manoeuvre, and even in the very formal construction of the Roman *testudo* the shields were not held so that they overlapped. Again, it is doubtful whether the men in the second rank, if indeed there were a second rank, would hold their shields over their own heads and the heads of those in the front rank; there would be too much risk of entanglement, one rank with another, in such a tight and solid formation. The first shock of battle was a hail of arrow and javelins from either side; it would be impossible to draw a bow or throw a javelin if the suggested formation were held. One can only believe that the army was ranged more or less in a line, with little space between each soldier, and that the shield was held in front of the body so that maximum protection was afforded to each man. This would give the impression to the opposing army of a wall composed of shields. Any second rank would hold the shield in the same way; when a warrior 'broke the shield-wall' he presumably fought his way through the line of shields.

The shield indeed played an important part in the battle: it took, or turned, arrows and javelins and sometimes became so weighed down with them that it had to be cast away; it acted as a defence in hand-to-hand fighting and, as in the poem quoted, was used to turn aside the spear thrust. We have many references in the literature to the orb being cut away and we must imagine that sometimes nothing was left in the hand but the boss which could then be used very effectively as a mailed fist – indeed there are references to the shield being used as a weapon of offence. After the battle it would be an easy matter to replace the broken orb.

The sword was used as a cutting weapon and the spear for thrusting, and the importance of these weapons is amply brought out in this poem which so well illuminates the art of war in the Anglo-Saxon period.

CHAPTER FIVE

Anglo-Saxon Art

THE origins of Anglo-Saxon art are threefold: insular Celtic, classical Mediterranean and Continental Germanic. Each influenced the growth of the national art, and the importance of each varied through the years. Sir Thomas Kendrick has described the art of Anglo-Saxon England before 900 as 'a series of conflicts between the mutually irreconcilable principles of the barbaric and classical aesthetic systems'; but perhaps it would be better described as a struggle for reconciliation between the two systems, a reconciliation that was achieved twice: first in the early eighth century and then again in the tenth and eleventh centuries. The history of Anglo-Saxon art is extremely complex and here I can only tackle it in a completely straightforward manner, showing simply its historical sequence and avoiding as many controversial elements as possible.

The clue to our understanding of Anglo-Saxon art lies in the fact that the barbaric artist abhorred naturalism as much as the classical artist of the Mediterranean abhorred the abstract. The Anglo-Saxon artist until the tenth century rarely attempted accurate portrayal of a human or animal form. He approached his subject in an abstract manner, breaking the surfaces and lines into a kaleidoscope of broken, twisted, tortuous and dismembered animal forms, which are completely divorced from the naturalism of his Mediterranean contemporary.

We must also bear in mind, in our discussion of the art of this people, the limited nature of the material that survives. For the first 250 years of the period under review our appreciation of the artistic achievement of the Anglo-Saxons is confined to the motifs which appear on jewellery and other similar articles of metal, stone or bone. There is no painting, no wood-carving or monumental art. From the last 350 years a considerable body of rather specialized painting and sculpture survives, which enables us to gain some idea of the richness of the art of this period; but the illuminated service books, Bibles, psalters and benedictionals which survive today do not tell us much about the wall paintings, stained glass windows and secular painting. Similarly, the memorial and preaching crosses, which are to be found in parish churches throughout the country, give no idea of the quality of the wood-carving and other plastic arts of the Anglo-Saxons. The surviving material, by its very nature, must give us a biased opinion of Anglo-Saxon art – our picture can never be complete – but where there is a tendency to condemn and say, 'There is no art', we should remember that our evidence is slight and unreliable.

PAGAN METALWORK AND JEWELLERY

The Anglo-Saxon artist broke slowly from the art of his Roman forerunner; it was not until well on in the fifth century that Anglo-Saxon art emerged as a separate entity based on its Germanic contemporaries. The first distinct style to emerge is found chiefly in Kent and the south-east and is known, because of its occurrence on a number of brooches, as 'the quoit-brooch style'. The chief motif [Fig. 31a] is a crouching quadruped seen in profile; the body, which has a double contour, is covered with slight incisions representing fur; occasionally it has spiral hips. The mouth is often open and the lips form an outward curved line. The style is executed in a lightly carved technique on a flat surface, and a polychrome effect is often given by gilding the metal if it is silver, or, if it is bronze, by inlaying it with sheet silver. In one instance, at Mucking, Essex, such animals [Fig. 31a] are seen on a large buckle of a provincial Roman military type and demonstrate the origin of the style in the art of the Roman world, for an aspect of the style is found, for example, on Roman spoons and elsewhere in Roman metalwork. Mrs Hawkes has suggested that the style was Jutish, *sensu strictu*, and that it had its origin in south Scandinavia. This theory has not been generally accepted and it seems more plausible to interpret the Scandinavian parallels to the Kentish style as having a common prototype with the Kentish material in the Roman world. If there is anything Germanic in this style (a theory suggested by other scholars) it must have been taken into the style well before the end of the Roman period as it appears on Roman table ware and on late Roman buckle plates. Whatever its origins, the style was adapted by Anglo-Saxon craftsmen of the early fifth century and used on a variety of objects.

The late Roman buckle, of which the Mucking piece is an elaborate example, was decorated in a method known as chip-carving, a technique used originally in the carving of hard-wood and adapted by the Romans to metalwork. A running lozenge pattern of conjoined Xs is marked out on the surface to be decorated; a corner of the chisel is then placed in the centre of the X and the wood is cut along the line of each leg so that the cut is deepest in the centre and just touches the surface at the end of the leg. The material, thus loosened by the chisel, is carved away so that, instead of an X marked on the surface, there is a pyramidal hole in its place.

To give a glittering effect to the surface this technique was adapted to metal casting by provincial Roman workshops, and a number of their products are found in Anglo-Saxon contexts [Pls. 30–32]. The technique began to influence the Germanic metalworker of southern Scandinavia who adapted non-geometrical motifs to this technique and gradually began to experiment with an animal style which was soon to spread throughout Western Europe. An early example of a non-Roman expression of this technique is to be seen on an early Anglo-Saxon object – perhaps made in this country, perhaps in Germany – an equal-armed brooch from Haslingfield, Cambridgeshire [Pl. 34]. The brooch has a chip-carved scroll ornament like that on the buckles, and backward-looking animals lying along its internal borders.

A considerable proportion of Anglo-Saxon metalwork in the fifth and sixth centuries was decorated with chip-carved ornament. The commonest ornament [Figs. 31b and c] during this period was an animal which, says Sir Thomas Kendrick, 'loses its zoological reality and is converted into mere pattern. Heads and legs, tails and teeth, are mixed together into an attractive pot-pourri of confusion which covers every square inch of the surface of the object.' This same decoration is encountered both in Germany and Scandinavia, as well as in Hungary and Eastern Europe. It is not easy to decide where this animal style, of which the Anglo-Saxon style is but a phase, first appeared, but it almost certainly received its immediate inspiration from south Scandinavia.

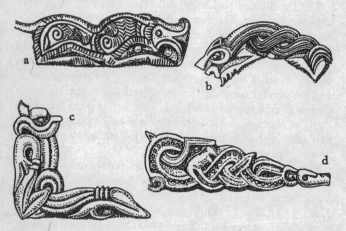

Fig. 31. Early Anglo-Saxon animal ornament: (a) animal of the quoit-brooch style from a buckle from Mucking, Essex; (b) and (c) animals of Style I from a saucer-brooch from Grave 46, Long Wittenham, Berks., and from a square-headed brooch from Suffolk; (d) animal of Style II from a drinking-horn mount from Taplow, Bucks.; (b–d after Davidson and Webster)

The style has been satisfactorily labelled by a Swedish scholar, Bernhard Salin, as 'Style I'. This term covers a number of varying forms of similar ornament here and abroad, but is still a highly satisfactory term for the English material. The style flourished from the end of the fifth to the late sixth century when it was replaced by another style (Style II) in which the restless movement of the first animal style, with its broken lines and abstract forms, was replaced [Fig. 31d] by a quieter, apparently simpler, ornament based on the interlacing and interplay of the ribbon-like bodies of animals and snakes. In effect the new art, sometimes known as the Ribbon Style, was not very far in its aims from the earlier disjointed art of the first style. The aim was still to cover the ornamented surface with complicated animal and tendril ornament. There was still no tendency to realism. Symmetry was used or ignored at will; on the Crundale Down sword

Fig. 32. Ribbon-style animal ornament, from the Sutton Hoo buckle and from a sword pommel from Crundale Down. London, British Museum

pommel [Fig. 32, right] symmetry is very strictly adhered to; on the great gold buckle from Sutton Hoo [Fig. 32, left] the structure of the buckle is symmetrical, but only the heads of the animals are placed symmetrically – their bodies wander off into tight, pleasing knots and into loose skilful loops all over the surface of the object. The origins of the Ribbon Style are obscure, but it was certainly not developed in England.

In this country there is an interesting fusion between the two styles, which is seen at its best on parts of the Taplow horn mounts – disjointed ornament of the first style is combined with the interlaced ornament of Style II. (Incidentally, it is interesting to note that both Style I and Style II, as well as the Fusion Style, all occur on different parts of the Taplow drinking-horn.) An interesting feature of the Style II, and one that can be seen on the clasp and buckle from Taplow [Pl. 44], is the combination of a false chip-carved effect with filigree wire. The false chip-carved effect is achieved by pressing gold and silver sheets into pitch, to produce a pattern similar to chip-carving, and capping the lines that stand up in relief with beaded wire.

One of the most important and striking elements in the art of the Anglo-Saxon pagan period is the rich polychrome jewellery of Kent and East Anglia. Polychrome jewellery is so called because it is inlaid with garnets, blue and green glass, niello and various white materials. There are two main types. The first is a rich, luxurious jewellery (Pl. 35) in which flat-cut stones and glass are set in gold or silver cells, built up from bands of metal on a base plate of gold or silver. (These cells give the polychrome jewellery another name, cloisonné, from the French *cloison* – a cell.) Another feature of this group of jewellery is panels of filigree-wire ornament which are spaced between the cells: filigree is also used to build up a border for the jewel. At the bottom of each cell a small piece of stamped foil is placed behind the garnet. These sheets, stamped in various patterns, abound in the Sutton Hoo jewellery, for instance, and serve to reflect the light back through the garnet at different angles to give a sparkling and lively effect to a stone which would otherwise be rather dull and flat. Some of the empty cells in the Wilton cross [Pl. 42] have lost their garnets but retained their foil.

The second class of polychrome jewellery is much humbler [Pls. 36, 37]; the base plate and cells are cast in one piece, as is the incidental ornament, which sometimes has a serrated edge in imitation of the filigree technique. These cells are filled with garnets; coloured glass rarely occurs. The borders of many of the objects in this class are decorated with small black rings of niello.

The objects most commonly executed in the polychrome manner are disc brooches which are usually found in Kent, but the technique in its application to other objects is well documented;

garnets, for example, quite frequently embellish the great square-headed brooches.

The shapes of the cells in the richer class of polychrome jewellery have been the basis for considerable discussion as to the origin of the technique. Most of the features of the Anglo-Saxon polychrome jewellery occur abroad in Italy, Sweden or the Low Countries. Although, generally speaking, the English material is of the highest quality, it would be extremely difficult to decide whether, for instance, the Wynaldum buckle-plate [Pl. 39], found recently in Holland, was made by a Dutch or an English craftsman or whether, in the words of Mr Bruce-Mitford, it was perhaps 'the work of a craftsman trained in Kent or Suffolk but working for a Continental patron'. Polychrome jewellery has its roots in the Gothic culture of the Black Sea area, where the craftsmen had perhaps inherited some of the techniques and skill of the Scythians. The great fourth-century treasure of Petrossa, Romania, and the Szilagy-Somlyo treasure from Hungary demonstrate the richness of the cloisonné technique in Eastern Europe, while, nearer home, the rich treasure (buried in 481) from Childeric's tomb found at Tournai, Belgium, gives us some idea of the high quality of the polychrome technique in Western Europe. The technique reached England, particularly Kent, from the Frankish area early in the sixth century. In its early stages the garnets are set in cast cells in disc and square-headed brooches [Pls. 36, 37] and in various other pieces of jewellery. Towards the end of the sixth century the true cloisonné jewellery began to be made in Kent and East Anglia and splendid objects like the Kingston brooch were created [Pl. 35]. The technique spread and continued in use throughout the greater part of the seventh century [e.g. Pls. 38, 40–42]. For much of this period Anglo-Saxon jewellery was of equal quality with that of the rest of Europe and on some occasions, as at Sutton Hoo [Pls. 1 and 4], is seen to achieve a brilliance without contemporary parallel.

Lastly, in our discussion of the art of the Anglo-Saxon pagan period, we must consider certain Celtic influences and motifs. Celtic motifs occur most commonly on the fairly large group of objects known as hanging-bowls [Pls. 43, 45], which are all, with two late exceptions, made of bronze and vary in diameter between 20 cm. and 45 cm.; they have at the rim three rings for suspension, clasped to the bowl by means of hooks which develop from an ornamental plaque. In later examples the plaques are often enamelled and another mount is attached inside the bowl on the bottom. These mounts are decorated in a curvilinear spiral style which has its roots in the native British Celtic ornament. The question of the hanging-bowl has already been discussed in relation to Sutton Hoo (p. 42). The bowls, however, are but one aspect of this revival of interest in Celtic forms and shapes. The boar which acts as a crest on the Benty Grange helmet [Pls. 28, 29] is in a direct line of descent from the large number of boars portrayed in a similar form by the pre-Roman Celts – boars are also depicted on the sword from the river Lark, which we have already mentioned, and on the Sutton Hoo epaulettes. In the field of human portraiture there are also some interesting Celtic connexions. The heads carved on the Sutton Hoo and Hough-on-the-Hill whetstones [Pl. 10], for example, are surely of Celtic origin and may have reached Anglo-Saxon art either through Scotland or Ireland. This Celtic repertoire passes full-bloodedly into Anglo-Saxon art. In the late seventh and eighth centuries we see these motifs used in the manuscripts, as well as on metal and bone objects. The developed spiral patterns, which appear in such a skilfully executed form in the Lindisfarne Gospels [Pl. 48], implicitly dated by inscription to about 700, are but developments of the ornamental motifs appearing on the Middleton Moor escutcheon [Pl. 43]. An ivory box [Fig. 7] of English manufacture from Gandersheim (now in the Ducal Museum, Brunswick) has an Anglo-Saxon animal style which is presumably of eighth-century date; but in the middle of the bottom of one side is a panel completely taken up by a developed spiral motif – one of its last definite occurrences in Anglo-Saxon art.

THE EFFECT OF CHRISTIANITY

All the art which we have discussed so far has been, with one or two exceptions, applied art, ornament on metal brooches and other objects of utility. The Church was to introduce into this country a completely new art form, painting, and was to re-kindle a dormant interest in monumental sculpture. These media were not immediately adopted, just as Christianity was not im-mediately adopted. No manuscripts written in England before the last half of the seventh century are known to survive and a similar statement could probably be made about Anglo-Saxon sculpture.

METALWORK: SEVENTH TO NINTH CENTURIES

It is often difficult for the professional archaeologist to remember that the Sutton Hoo cenotaph, essentially such a pagan pheno-menon, was laid down thirty or forty years after the Augustinian mission, and that most of the jewellery found at Sutton Hoo, and indeed most of the metalwork ornamented in Style II, was pro-bably made after the official introduction of Christianity into this country. It must be stressed that the introduction of Christianity did not put an end to the work of the pagan Anglo-Saxon jeweller. We have seen how he adapted his craft to making such Christian objects as the pectoral cross of St Cuthbert [Pl. 40] and other associated crosses. The metalworker merely changed his religion because he considered it politic and continued to work in the tradition of his masters and his forefathers, developing his art and broadening his repertoire. Naturally he was in-fluenced by the newly introduced arts, but he continued to work with the familiar forms. The last fling of the polychrome jeweller's use of garnet is to be seen in the garnets he placed at the terminals of the trefoil mount found in the Kirkoswald hoard [Pl. 62]. But the strength of the chip-carving tradition is to be seen on the Witham pins [Pl. 55], where the glittering gilt bronze emphasizes the animals, skilfully interlaced in a new and

Fig. 33. Animal ornament from the Witham pins. Much enlarged.
(See plate 55)

more naturalistic development of Style II. It should not be
thought that animals were the only motifs used by the Anglo-
Saxon artist of this period; scroll patterns are to be seen, for
instance, on the Kirkoswald brooch and the use of foliage motifs
is particularly marked. Occasionally the animals degenerated
into foliage, as for example on the ring found a few years ago
at Poslingford in Suffolk [Fig. 34].

Chip-carved gilt bronze, as a technique, was replaced, towards the end of the eighth century by carved silver, sometimes
inlaid with black niello or gold plates [Pl. 64]; the animals and
other ornamental motifs were defined by shallow carving and
speckled all over with the corner of an engraving tool. The designs were, of course, marked out on the metal before being
carved and these lines of construction can be seen on a number
of objects. Sometimes the artist would try out his patterns and
his animals on a piece of bone, as for example that found in the
last century in York, before carving them in silver [Pl. 67].
Among the best examples of this style of silver work are certain

Fig. 34. Extended drawing of the ornament on the gold ring from Poslingford, Suffolk. London, British Museum

mounts from a hoard from Trewhiddle in Cornwall [Pl. 63], which has given its name to the style [Fig. 35].

The skill of the Anglo-Saxon metalworker of the Christian period was renowned throughout Europe. In Rome, Anglo-Saxon craftsmen of the *Schola Saxonum* were making vessels for the altar of St Peter's itself. When Duke Tassilo of Austria founded the monastery of Kremsmünster in the year 777, he gave to the abbey at least one piece of plate, a chalice [Pl. 61], which bears his name, and which was almost certainly made by a craftsman trained in England or in an Anglo-Carolingian School. The glittering gilt chip-carved surface of this object bears charming interlaced animals and foliate motifs of English origin, as well as portraits of Christ and the Apostles which are of Mediterranean influence; the animal ornament cannot be exactly paralleled in this country, but its style is so close to that of England that it must be seen as an Anglo-Continental style [Fig. 36]. The English styles also influenced Irish and Scottish metalworkers, then at the height of their powers. The animal patterns of the Kells crozier, for example, are extremely close to those of the Trewhiddle hoard, while some of the animal ornament in the St Ninian's Isle, Shetland, hoard is derived from the rather earlier Anglo-Saxon animal ornament, best seen in manuscript in the Lindisfarne Gospels. This style was then in the main-stream of European art. Its highest achievements are seen in such objects as the Fuller brooch [Pl. 65], which is fine enough to stand beside any of the world's great jewellery. The eighth and ninth centuries form one of the greatest periods in the art of the Anglo-Saxon metalworker: his command of his medium is well illustrated by the sword pommel from Fetter Lane in the City of London [Pl. 24] with its niello and parcel-gilt animal and leaf pattern, or by the object perhaps made at the command of King Alfred – the Alfred Jewel [Pls. 57, 58], one of the chief treasures of the University of Oxford.

The Alfred Jewel, now in the Ashmolean Museum, which was found in 1693 in Newton Park, near the Island of Athelney

Fig. 35. Animal ornament from horn mount, Trewhiddle, Cornwall. (See plate 63)

in Somerset, is of gold with a crystal plaque covering the enam-elled figure of a man holding two sceptres. The terminal takes the form of an animal's head and an Anglo-Saxon inscription round the edge reads, + AELFRED MEC HEHT GEWYRCAN (Alfred ordered me to be made). The back-plate is engraved with

Fig. 36. German, Irish and English animal ornament compared: (a) from the Tassilo Chalice; (b) the Kells crozier and (c) Trewhiddle horn mount.

an elaborate foliate design which has Carolingian as well as Anglo-Saxon affinities. The animal-head terminal, which is executed in filigree wire and in granules of gold, must originally have been riveted to a wooden or ivory handle or staff. The use of the jewel is not known; its only parallel, apparently, is the Minster Lovell jewel [Pl. 59], which is also preserved in the Ashmolean Museum at Oxford. These jewels are two of the rare examples from the late Saxon period of the technique of cloisonné enamel: another English example is the circular brooch from Dowgate Hill [Pl. 60], with its representation of a nimbed or crowned figure, which is very close in style to the portrait in the Alfred Jewel.

MANUSCRIPTS: SEVENTH TO NINTH CENTURIES

At the end of the ninth century new motifs make themselves felt in the art of the metalworker, but for the moment we must retrace our steps and consider the other art forms practised by the Christian Anglo-Saxons. The Church brought to the pagan English the skill of writing and illuminating books. The illuminators had three sources for their art. From Mediterranean illumination the Anglo-Saxons borrowed the idea of naturalistic representation of the human figure, and certain other formulae of illumination, as, for example, the use of arcading to contain the canon tables (a concordance of references to corresponding passages in the different Gospels). From Ireland probably came such features as the elaborate initials, particularly that which occurs in the eighteenth verse of Chapter I of St Matthew's

Gospel, *Christi autem generatio sic erat* ('Now the birth of Christ was on this wise'). From the native Anglo-Saxon art came the use of elaborate ribbon interlace and animal ornament, together with the idea of covering whole pages with ornament to produce the so-called 'carpet pages'. There are, of course, many nuances within this rather simplified scheme of origins, and as the ancient barbaric spirit of the Anglo-Saxon gained the upper hand, so the direct Mediterranean influences became more obscure in the art of the scribe and the three influences fused into one characteristic Anglo-Saxon style.

The earliest surviving illuminated manuscript of Anglo-Saxon origin is the Book of Durrow [Pl. 46] which, although once thought to be of Irish origin, is now accepted by many scholars as a Northumbrian work. It dates from the last half of the seventh century and was probably written within a few years of 675. The purely decorative ornament of this book is completely in keeping with the insular ornament of the Ribbon Style and with such Celtic features as spiral patterns of a form found on the hanging-bowl escutcheons. The symbols of the Evangelists, which act as a frontispiece to each gospel, make no concession to naturalism at all and are far removed from their Mediterranean prototypes, yet they are drawn with remarkable clarity. Similarity of style between certain motifs from the Book of Durrow and the enamelled hanging-bowl escutcheons is surely significant where the colour of the book is concerned. The reds and yellows of this book are the colours of the more or less contemporary enamels, and more direct parallels to enamelling are to be seen on the figure of one of the evangelist symbols, whose robe is decorated with a pattern which imitates millefiori work. The ornament of the Book of Durrow has its background in pagan Anglo-Saxon art. The great decorative pages of Durrow have been compared with the rectangular panels of the Sutton Hoo shoulder clasps, and parallels drawn between the animal ornament of Durrow and that of Sutton Hoo. One of the new decorative elements, plain ribbon interlace, which first appears in the Book of Durrow, is of frequent occurrence in the later Anglo-Saxon art and makes its first appearance here.

Written and illuminated in Northumbria, shortly after the

Book of Durrow, is a small group of manuscripts [Pls. 47–50] of which the three most important are the Codex Amiatinus, the Lindisfarne Gospels and the Echternach Gospels. They were all produced within a few years of the turn of the seventh century. Two of these books, the Lindisfarne Gospels and the Echternach Gospels, continue in the insular tradition of the Book of Durrow, bringing it, however, to a perfection never before attained. The third book [Pl. 47], known as the Codex Amiatinus (now in the Laurentian Library at Florence), was one of the three copies of the Gospels ('*tres pandectes novae translationis*', as Bede describes them) written at the command of the first Abbot of Jarrow (Ceolfrith, died 716), one for the monastery of Monkwearmouth, one for the monastery of Jarrow and one for the Pope. Ceolfrith himself set out to deliver it in person, but on the way he died at Langres in France and the book had to be taken to Rome by his followers. The book was apparently modelled on one of those brought from Italy by Benedict Biscop and is entirely Italianate in the character of its illumination. It is influenced only in a very minor way by the artistic traditions of Northumbria, which is rather surprising when one considers that, at the same time as the Codex Amiatinus was made, only a few miles away on a small island off the coast of Northumberland, the Lindisfarne Gospels [Pls. 48, 49] were being written and illuminated in a markedly Anglo-Saxon style by Eadfrith (Bishop of Lindisfarne 698–721). Recent studies have suggested that it was written and illuminated within a year or two of 698. This book, which is probably one of the finest works of art ever produced in England, synthesizes in its many illuminated pages the artistic traditions of three worlds, the Mediterranean, the Celtic North and Anglo-Saxon England. The four portraits of the Evangelists, for example, are based on Italian prototypes tautened by the economy of line of the insular scribe. The controlled exuberance of the inter-laced animals in the carpet pages, with the jewel-like quality of their painting, is purely Anglo-Saxon. The animals are similar in certain respects to those on the Witham pins [Pl. 55] which, although much simpler, glitter in a manner that may be com-pared to the glow attained by the illuminator. The third of this group of manuscripts, the Echternach Gospels, which bears a cousinly relationship to the Lindisfarne Gospels without being quite so grand, was painted in Northumbria, probably (according to Professor Brown) in the same scriptorum as the Lindisfarne Gospels, and was sent shortly afterwards to the newly founded German monastery of Echternach, where it became a model for a style of illumination which grew up there and which had its roots in Northumbria.

These great painted manuscripts of the late seventh and early eighth centuries obscure, with their brilliance, their more humble successors of the period between 725 and 850. Certain manuscripts, such as the Book of Chad [Pl. 51] in the Library of Lichfield Cathedral, continue the native Anglo-Saxon tradition of Durrow and Echternach, just as the great school of manuscripts painted, probably at Canterbury, between the middle of the eighth and the middle of the ninth century, retain many of the traits of the Lindisfarne group, while gradually taking into their ornamental repertoire the Continental motifs and ornaments of the Carolingian Renaissance. Two of the richest of these manuscripts are the Codex Aureus of the Royal Library in Stockholm and a Gospel book [Pl. 52] in the British Museum (Royal 1.E.VI). The great pages of purple vellum in these manuscripts give an impression of luxury and richness which is marred, in the case of Royal 1.E.VI at least, by the fact that the silver lettering has oxidized and obscured the brilliance of the painting. The portraits of the Evangelists and the frames round them in this Gospel book can be compared with those of such Carolingian manuscripts as the Godescalc Evangeliar, while the canon tables retain much of the incidental detail that was used in the Lindisfarne Gospels. However, in one of the earlier manuscripts of the school, the Canterbury Psalter in the British Museum, the frame which surrounds the portrait of David is of a completely Celtic character. The arch under which he sits, surrounded by his musicians, is composed of spirals of the type found on the hanging-bowls, while the columns which support the arch have an interlace ornament not unlike that of the Lindisfarne Gospels. This same Psalter and the Stockholm Codex Aureus have many minor illuminated initials, including, in the case of the former, initials which contain scenes illustrating

Biblical happenings, a feature which occurs here for the first time and which was to be persistently popular throughout English medieval illumination. It is interesting, incidentally, to note that the richest and latest of this group of manuscripts, Royal 1.E.VI, contains no illuminated initials. Even in these books the metal-worker's techniques are seen to be carried into the manuscript art: small speckled animals are reserved against a black background in a manner which imitates the silver and niello art of the Trewhiddle style. The Canterbury School succeeded the Northumbrian School as the centre of English painting because of the difficult and troublous political situation in the north; it, in turn, was to be eclipsed in very much the same way by the Viking incursions into England. King Alfred's lamentations concerning the fall in the standard of learning in England, with which he prefaced his translation of Gregory's *Cura Pastoralis*, are reflected in the lack of late ninth-century manuscripts illuminated and written in England.

SCULPTURE: SEVENTH TO NINTH CENTURIES

The development of manuscript art in England was paralleled, on a lesser plane, by monumental sculpture. Of this group of monuments Sir Thomas Kendrick, writing in 1938, said: 'No department of our national antiquities is more urgently in need of organized study than the English crosses ... it [is] an excessively embarrassing fact that the principal problems of chronology and stylistic development are not likely to be solved before a complete survey of the material has been accomplished.' In 1970 every word of this trenchant remark is still true. The survey initiated by Kendrick has never been completed and, although work continues, we can expect no published survey for at least ten years. Any chronological judgements must be made purely stylistically – an extremely dangerous thing to do. Here I can draw only the broad outlines of a hazy subject.

The origin of the Anglo-Saxon sculptural tradition is obscure. The memorial stones of sixth- and early seventh-century date from western and northern Britain do not seem to have influenced the Anglo-Saxon sculptor, and it is reasonable to suppose that sculpture came to England with Christianity from the Mediterranean, primarily as architectural embellishment. Only later (towards the end of the seventh century) were free-standing pieces of sculpture set up in the form of memorial or preaching crosses. Such monuments seem to be an Anglo-Saxon innovation, for nowhere else in Europe or the British Isles are there undoubtedly earlier examples of great stone crosses. Although architectural sculpture continued to flourish, by far the most remarkable examples of the sculptor's art are the crosses.

The most accomplished school of Anglo-Saxon carving in the seventh and eighth centuries appears to have been Northumbrian. Indeed the quality of the carving can broadly be said to follow the geographical trends of manuscript illumination: for towards the end of the eighth century Mercia and southern England appear to have produced the greater works of art, so much so that, when in the early tenth century there was a revival of stone carving in the north, the first products were crude and ham-fisted. The assembled corpus of Anglo-Saxon sculpture is so large that it is impossible to do justice to it in the space at my disposal. I intend therefore to describe certain pieces of exceptional quality and discuss them in their general context.

The most outstanding piece of Northumbrian sculpture is the 5·5 m. cross from Ruthwell in Dumfriesshire [Pl. 53], which has been mentioned in an earlier chapter (p. 54); it should probably be thought of in the same chronological context as the Lindisfarne and Echternach Gospels. The four arms of the cross originally bore portraits of the four Evangelists but only two arms survive. Below the head of the cross, on each of the broader faces of the shaft, are various Christian scenes: John the Baptist, Our Lord in Majesty, Paul and Anthony in the desert, the Flight into Egypt, the Visitation, Mary Magdalene washing Christ's feet, the Annunciation and the Crucifixion. The sides of the shaft bear an elaborate vine-scroll peopled with animals and birds, the whole motif known technically as an 'inhabited vine-scroll'. The scenes on the two faces and the panels on the sides of the cross are surrounded by plain borders, those on the sides bearing a rendering in runic lettering of one of the most beautiful of all the Anglo-Saxon poems, *The Dream of the Rood*. The borders of the pictorial panels bear Latin inscriptions describing the scenes depicted. The figure-carving on this cross was done by an artist who was more than usually competent in his medium: the carvings are deep, soft and full, and the features are portrayed with a naturalism rarely found in an Anglo-Saxon artist's work; yet that this was carved by an Anglo-Saxon sculptor cannot be doubted. There is a stiffness present that no Mediterranean-trained artist would have allowed. Kendrick has pointed out the awkwardness of the Mary Magdalene scene where the woman is so contorted as to be almost gross, while the drapery lacks the flow of any Mediterranean counterpart. Nearly every other example of Northumbrian sculpture, however, is more clumsy or less naturalistic than the Ruthwell cross. The Bewcastle cross, for instance, which may well have been modelled on the Ruthwell cross, has, in its portrayal of the human figures, more abstract or insular characteristics than the other possesses. Although similar panels of Biblical scenes are very popular in Northumbrian crosses, in many cases they become secondary to panels which contain abstract designs of interlaced animals and vine-scrolls, 'inhabited' or otherwise.

Southern English art at the end of the eighth century was very much under the influence of the style of ornament typified in the Trewhiddle hoard and in the manuscript B.M. Royal 1.E.VI [Pls. 52, 63, Fig. 35]. Traces of sculpture in southern England belonging to an earlier period are apparently rare, although the one important exception of the Reculver cross fragments must be mentioned. There is a reasonable possibility that these few miserable fragments are all that survive of a magnificent cross of seventh-century date: archaeological evidence, based on excavation, seems to support this theory. The fragments themselves show the cross to have been round-shafted, bearing figural scenes which were surrounded in part by ribbon interlace. There is a delicacy about the carving that is not met with elsewhere in Anglo-Saxon sculptural art, but the pieces are unfortunately too fragmentary to be placed definitely in any context. For the rest, such Anglo-Saxon carving as is found in Mercia and southern England is very much influenced by the Northumbrian styles and by the art of the manuscripts. The cross-head from Cropthorne, Worcestershire [Pl. 66], for example, bears an animal which is closely related to the ones in the manuscript Royal 1.E.VI, while at the same time the birds and foliate ornament are direct descendants of the Northumbrian inhabited vine-scroll. The Cropthorne cross-head is one of the higher achievements of southern Anglo-Saxon sculptural art of the ninth century, most of the surviving sculpture of this period and area being flat and undistinguished; it is not until the tenth century that the sculpture of Wessex and the south rises to its greatest heights.

It would not be fitting to leave the subject of Anglo-Saxon sculpture without some reference to two examples of Northumbrian carving which stand by themselves, removed from the art of the monumental sculptor. The first is the oak coffin of St Cuthbert [Pl. 54] which was apparently made in 698. It is carved with linear representations of the Evangelists, the Apostles, the Archangels, etc., in a style similar to the Evangelist portraits in the Lindisfarne Gospels. Professor Kitzinger has shown that the figures have their stylistic origin on the Continent, in the same way that the Evangelist figures in the Echternach/Lindisfarne group have Continental connexions, and that they are best paralleled in this country on the Ruthwell cross. The second piece of Northumbrian carving [Pl. 56] which must be mentioned is the Franks Casket (so called after Sir Augustus Franks, Keeper of the Department of British Antiquities in the British Museum 1866–96, who gave it to the museum). It is of whalebone and is carved with scenes, taken from a universal history, of such diverse subjects as Wayland the Smith, the Capture of Jerusalem by Titus and the Adoration of the Magi. The whole of the box, each side of which is framed by a runic inscription, is carved with a barbaric abandon which is far removed from the slightly barbarized classicism of the Lindisfarne Evangelist portraits, the figures of the Ruthwell cross and the carvings of St Cuthbert's coffin. The casket stands by itself as an expression of the vernacular art of the early eighth century. These two pieces are important in so far as they are two of the very few objects which survive in such perishable materials, and serve to remind us that our knowledge of Anglo-Saxon art is very one-sided.

THE TENTH-CENTURY RENAISSANCE

After Alfred's Viking wars came a period of political consolidation which involved a series of campaigns against the Vikings, and it is with the accession of Edgar in 959 and with the monastic reforms of Oswald, Dunstan and Æthelwold, that England, and with it English art, achieved another period of greatness. Indeed, it might be possible to think of the late ninth and early tenth centuries as a period barren of artistic merit, if it were not for two objects: the stole and maniple [Pl. 68] found in the coffin of St Cuthbert.

Very little is known about English embroidery in the Anglo-Saxon period, but literary references indicate its high quality. It is recorded, for example, that when William the Conqueror returned from a visit to England in the middle of the eleventh century, his Norman subjects were astonished by the quality of the robes he had acquired in England. Later, in the twelfth century, embroideries of 'English work' (*opus anglicanum*) were to become famous throughout Europe. Inscriptions on the stole and maniple of St Cuthbert imply that they were made, probably at Winchester, between 909 and 916. The figural subjects embroidered on them have already been described (p. 58). The elongated figures are executed with remarkable sensitivity; they wear loosely draped clothes, their stance is well balanced and naturalistic, and their faces are by no means stereotyped. The figures are separated from each other by stiff, formal acanthus leaves. They are embroidered in blues, greens, pinks and browns and set against a golden background: the whole effect is one of extreme richness. The only other surviving English embroidery of this period is a fragment in the Basilica Ambrosiana in Milan, although early ninth-century fragments are recorded from Norway and Belgium.

These pieces demonstrate that, in the south of England at least, the sophisticated classes were turning to the Continent for artistic inspiration. The style of the stole and maniple of St Cuthbert is completely Carolingian and its ultimate origin is Byzantine: there is no trace of any insular stylistic trends. The poverty-stricken state of English art before the middle of the tenth century is reflected in all its forms, except only these few embroideries which are so Carolingian in their conception. In metalwork and sculpture the artist was struggling to attain the brilliance of his insular predecessors in the face of an influx of Scandinavian taste; and in the field of manuscript illumination the artist attempted to keep alive the English ninth-century art while trying, at the same time, to adopt Continental models. The fleshy Carolingian acanthus leaf and the decorated initials with their native Anglo-Saxon traditions do achieve competence, but never brilliance, in such manuscripts as the Junius Psalter (the Bodleian Library, Oxford) and, from Durham, the Life of St Cuthbert (Corpus Christi College, Cambridge).

MANUSCRIPTS FROM EDGAR TO THE CONQUEST

In the middle of the tenth century, however, a brilliant style of manuscript illumination of the highest quality was introduced, based on the Continental models which people like Dunstan had got to know during their visits, enforced or otherwise, to France. These manuscripts are said to belong to the 'Winchester School', but it is important to realize that other places besides Winchester had *scriptoria* which were every bit as competent.

The grandest and most important of these manuscripts is the Benedictional of St Æthelwold, now in the British Museum, which was painted in Winchester between 971 and 984. This most sumptuous of late Anglo-Saxon books is only paralleled by a pontifical, also painted in Winchester, known as the Benedictional of Robert of Jumièges (now in the Bibliothèque Municipale of Rouen). A Latin poem at the beginning of the Benedictional of St Æthelwold records the decoration of the book as well as its writing: 'He (Æthelwold) commanded also to be made in this book many frames well adorned and filled with various figures decorated with numerous beautiful colours and with gold.' The chief glory of the book is the decorative frames which overwhelm both the text and the miniatures. Here can be seen the Anglo-Saxon artist's inherent attraction to ornament for the sake of ornament, which was so noticeable a feature of earlier manuscripts. The lush Carolingian acanthus spills out of the frame into the centre of the page and into the borders. In some cases the borders are slightly more restrained and one can appreciate more readily the ability of the artist as the portrayer of the human form. In the representation of the Annunciation [Pl. 69] for example, we see an angel amid swirling draperies drawn with confidence and sensitivity. The manuscript is coloured in a highly extravagant fashion; pastel shades are blended and contrasted with rich colours – purples, golds, greens and blues.

In the early years of the eleventh century there was still a considerable amount of liveliness exemplified by the Winchester artist who illuminated a *de luxe* copy of the charter originally granted to the New Minster by King Edgar in 966 [Pl. 70]. The style survived the Norman Conquest but was soon overwhelmed by the new international Romanesque.

But there is another major tradition which is to be seen in the Anglo-Saxon manuscripts of the tenth and eleventh centuries – a tradition based on the art of the French school of Rheims. One mid ninth-century manuscript, the Utrecht Psalter (written at Hautevillers, near Rheims), is of particular importance in the history of later Anglo-Saxon drawing. That it is difficult to underestimate the importance of this style in tenth- and eleventh-century English art is demonstrated by the copy of the Utrecht Psalter [Pl. 71] in the British Museum, which was made in southern England (probably at St Augustine's, Canterbury) about 1000, and which reproduces all the breathless activity of the original. The style of drawing is impressionistic; the figures tend to be spindly and their protruding eyes, hunched backs and twisted forms, together with the swirling draperies, are executed with simple quick strokes of the pen. There is perhaps a more linear quality about the copy than is to be found in the original, but there is the same sense of movement and light. This style was not intended to be used in the lush manuscripts of the Winchester School, but its effect is felt there, as can perhaps be seen in the New Minster Charter. It is more easily seen in the series of scientific books of which a fairly large number have survived.

Towards the end of the eleventh century the style, though still influencing English drawing, becomes more angular, while the quickly drawn figures, with their flickering quality, are reduced to more stylized, though successful, forms.

Anglo-Saxon manuscript art of this late period, then, was influenced by two Continental traditions. The first was the formalized Carolingian art, which developed into the masterly, luxurious, individual style of Winchester, and the second, the light, airy, impressionistic style of the school of Rheims, typified by the Utrecht Psalter.

SCULPTURE FROM ALFRED TO THE CONQUEST

The sculpture of the period falls into two distinct groups, that which follows the Winchester traditions and that which develops in Northumbria, based on the old vine-scroll and interlace patterns and on new Viking taste. Examples of the former are rare, while examples of the latter, although numerous, often seem to be, in the words of Kendrick, 'a vast and dreary assemblage of carvings that are of indifferent quality or downright bad'.

In the south-west of England about twenty fragments of stone sculpture, influenced by the Winchester style, survive. The angels in the small church at Bradford-on-Avon [Pl. 73], the 'Harrowing of Hell' scene in Bristol Cathedral and the Inglesham Crucifixion are the most famous. The draperies of these carvings are even stiffer than those of the contemporary manuscripts, while their portraiture, where it can be seen beneath the weathering, is coarse and stereotyped. The sculptures, however, are not without distinction, as technically they are well executed. The angel from the rood in the church of St Lawrence at Bradford-on-Avon, for example, is a very competent rendering in stone of the similar motif in the New Minster Charter [Pl. 70], with which it must be more or less contemporary. But none of this sculpture is really brilliant. The nearest thing to brilliancy is achieved in ivory carvings, as, for example, on a triangular ivory plaque from Winchester [Pl. 75] which has much of the quality of the linear Winchester manuscripts converted into the round.

In the north of England the sculptures continue the tradition of the memorial and preaching crosses of the earlier period. The new Viking taste is reflected in the subjects which appear on them. At Halton in Lancashire, for instance, parts of the Scandinavian Sigurd Saga are represented. It was this Viking taste which built up a sculptural style which only achieved success when it was re-exported to Denmark – where it is known to archaeologists as the Jellinge Style. That the crude designs on the multitude of stones from the North could have blossomed into anything as accomplished as the Danish Jellinge Style seems incredible. The Vikings brought back to Northumbria a taste for animal ornament – the animals that were produced were grotesque and ugly in the extreme. A cross from Middleton, Yorkshire, for example, bears an animal that lacks any charm but that of extreme naïvety. As with all these later Northern

Fig. 37. Stone cross from Middleton, Yorkshire

crosses, the technique is strictly two-dimensional : there is never any attempt to carve in the round or to give any impression of depth.

The sculpture of Mercia and eastern England shows a continuation of the same dull carving that occurs in the North – an interesting development is the round-shafted crosses of Mercia. The Northumbrian styles even had an effect in the South; one of the crosses from Ramsbury, Wiltshire, for example, and a cross from All Hallows' Church, London, demonstrate that certain sculptors were working in a style akin to that used in the north of England.

However, one exciting monumental style did develop in England as a result of the mingling of Viking and English art, a style which is best illustrated by the vivacious tombstone from the churchyard of St Paul's Cathedral, London [Pl. 74]. Here we have a great animal carved in low relief, in a modification of the Viking Ringerike Style, charging across the stone with its head turned backwards in a flurry of zoomorphic tendril scrolls: the whole was painted and the body of the animal covered in small dots (successor perhaps of the speckled animal of the ninth century). Its great claw-like feet, its small head, its spiral hips and the long tendril with the tiny curled end are typical of an English application of a Viking art which influenced English sculpture and metalwork and even made itself felt in a small number of manuscripts. The stone dates from the early years of the eleventh century, presumably from the period when England was part of the Danish Empire. This style has a life and vitality of its own which, at its best on the St Paul's slab, is breath-taking.

In an English version of the same style is an ivory comb in the British Museum [Pls. 76, 77]. On one side of this comb is a carving of an interlaced animal in the Ringerike style, with two cat-like animals on the reverse side, whose heads are paralleled in both manuscripts and metal objects of the same period (cf. Pl. 79).

THE ART OF THE METALWORKER: 900–1066

It is fitting that we should end this chapter, as we began it, with the art of the metalworker, for even at this late period metal was one of the materials the Anglo-Saxon artist could best handle. Unfortunately the richest pieces of metalwork made in this period do not survive, and we have only a series of minor objects which reflect, rather than illustrate, the glory of English metalwork. The great gold and silver figures that appear in the inventories have been melted down and all that survives is a handful of brooches and knick-knacks, and a few crude pieces of church plate. Even the richest piece of all, the gold and silver brooch from the King's School, Canterbury, is of second-rate workmanship, with clumsy degenerate animal ornament carried out in the tradition of the Trewhiddle animals in silver against a niello background. The same niello background also occurs on a pair of shrine plates in the British Museum, bearing crudely executed animals which, while reflecting the form of the Trewhiddle animals, demonstrate the artist's struggle with the new Viking styles of Jellinge and Ringerike. The Anglo-Saxon metalworker's mastery of the Ringerike Style can be seen again in a rather crude form on a brooch from Sutton, Isle of Ely [Pl. 78], found in the late seventeenth century with a hoard of coins of William the Conqueror. The animal and snake patterns in the four central fields of this object are quite skilful adaptations, by a second-rate craftsman, of a Viking style, tempered with the grotesque element so beloved of English artists through the ages.

The Winchester style also appears in the metalwork, and

Fig. 38. Animal ornament on a tenth-century Anglo-Saxon shrine plate in the British Museum

particularly in a small group of bronzes which bear all the ornamental elements of the manuscripts, including foliage and grotesque animals. This can be seen on the censer cover from Canterbury [Pl. 79], with its addorsed birds in openwork, standing on acanthus leaves in the true manner of the Winchester Style. The figural style of the Winchester manuscripts is also to be seen in metal on such pieces as the portable altar [Pl. 16], now in the Cluny Museum, which has been described elsewhere (p. 57).

This book, which has attempted to sketch the story of Anglo-Saxon England as seen through the eyes of the archaeologist, finishes with a discussion of Anglo-Saxon art. English art is often underestimated, even by Englishmen. During the centuries between the fall of Rome and the coming of the Normans, English art achieved greatness on a number of occasions and the art historian can point to features of modern English art which betray distinct characteristics of Anglo-Saxon art.

It is not only the art of the Anglo-Saxons, however, which influences us today; much of modern English life stems directly from Anglo-Saxon roots. Our administrative machinery (both local and national), our laws, our parliament, our language and our literature are ultimately Anglo-Saxon in origin. They have changed through the centuries to such an extent that the Anglo-Saxon of Alfred's reign would barely recognize them, but their origins are clear enough to the historian. More tangible reminders of the Englishman's Anglo-Saxon heritage abound – the majority of English place-names were coined in this period, as were some of our personal names; the ground-plans of many of our villages and even a few of our towns were laid down by the Anglo-Saxons. The boundaries of our parishes, the broad lines of the county system, and even the method of dating historical events from the birth of Christ, are Anglo-Saxon in origin. Viking warriors, Norman kings, French administrators, German royalty, French Protestants and Central European political refugees have all been absorbed into an English nation which remains basically Anglo-Saxon.

Book List

MUCH of the material used in this book is drawn from short papers published in many journals of varying degree of obscurity. It would be impossible to refer to all these papers here; I have therefore listed the principal books which I have used as sources. Such original sources as the *Anglo-Saxon Chronicle*, which were actually written during the Anglo-Saxon period, are missing from the bibliography but will be found in Miss Whitelock's volume of *English Historical Documents* (cited below). The best histories of the period are those by Collingwood and Myres (for the early period) and by Stenton (for the later period). In illustration of the last chapter of the book the reader is further referred to an excellent series of colour slides of manuscripts and jewellery, published by The Colour Centre, Farnham Royal, Slough, Bucks., which give a brilliant idea of the technical and aesthetic qualities of the art of this period.

The use of this book list will provide a bibliography for most Anglo-Saxon subjects. The reader is, however, referred to the following journals, recent numbers of which contain important articles on Anglo-Saxon subjects: *The Journal of the British Archaeological Association, The Archaeological Journal, Archaeologia,* and, more especially, *The Antiquaries Journal, Medieval Archaeology* and *British Archaeological Abstracts.*

ÅBERG, N., *The Anglo-Saxons in England*, Uppsala, 1926.

ÅBERG, N., *The Occident and the Orient in the Art of the Seventh Century*, Stockholm, 1943–7.

BALDWIN-BROWN, G., *The Arts in Early England*, 6 vols., 1903–37,

BARLOW, F., *The English Church 1000–1066*, London, 1963.

BATTISCOMBE, C. F. (ed.), *The Relics of Saint Cuthbert*, Oxford, 1956.

BLAIR, P. H., *An Introduction to Anglo-Saxon England*, Cambridge, 1956.

BONSER, W., *An Anglo-Saxon and Celtic Biography*, Oxford, 1957.

British Museum Guide to Anglo-Saxon and Foreign Teutonic Antiquities, London, 1923.

BRØGGER, A. W. and SHETELIG, H., *The Viking Ships*, Oslo, 1951.

BRØNSTED, J., *Early English Ornament*, London-Copenhagen, 1924

BRUCE-MITFORD, R. L. S., *The Sutton Hoo Ship Burial, A Handbook*, London, 1968.

CLAPHAM, A. W., *English Romanesque Architecture before the Conquest*, Oxford, 1930.

CLAPHAM, J. H. and POWER, E. *et al.*, *The Cambridge Economic History of Europe*, Cambridge, 1941–52.

CLARK, J. G. D., *Prehistoric Europe; the Economic Basis*, London, 1952.

COLLINGWOOD, R. G. and MYRES, J. N. L., *Roman Britain and the English Settlements*, Oxford, 1936.

DAVIDSON, H. R. E., *The Sword in Anglo-Saxon England*, London, 1962.

DOLLEY, R. H. M. (ed), *Anglo-Saxon Coins*, London, 1961.

DOLLEY, R. H. M., *The Hiberno-Norse coins in the British Museum*, London, 1966.

EVISON, V. I., *The Fifth-century Invasion South of the Thames*, London, 1965.

FAUSSETT, B., *Inventorium Sepulchrale*, London, 1856.

GODFREY, C. J., *The Church in Anglo-Saxon England*, Cambridge, 1962.

GORDON, E. V., *The Battle of Maldon*, London, 1937.

GRABAR, A. and NORDENFALK, C., *Early Medieval Painting*, Lausanne, 1957.

HARDEN, D. B. (ed), *Dark Age Britain*, London, 1956.

HASELOFF, G., *Der Tassilokelch*, Munich, 1951.

HODGKIN, R. K., *A History of the Anglo-Saxons*, 2 vols. (3rd ed.), Oxford, 1952.

HOLLISTER, C. W., *Anglo-Saxon Military Institutions*, Oxford, 1962.

HOLMQVIST, W., *Germanic Art*, Stockholm, 1955.

HOSKINS, W. G., *The Making of the English Landscape*, 1955.

JESSEN, K. and HELBAEK, H., *Cereals in Great Britain and Ireland in Prehistoric and Early Historic Times*, Copenhagen, 1944.

KELLER, M. L., *The Anglo-Saxon Weapon Names* (Anglistische Forschungen, 15), Heidelberg, 1906.

KENDRICK, T. D., *Anglo-Saxon Art to 900*, London, 1938.

KENDRICK, T. D., *Late Saxon and Viking Art*, London, 1949.

KENDRICK, T. D. *et al.*, *Codex Lindisfarnensis*, Oltun-Lausanne, 1960.

KIRK, J., *The Alfred and Minster Lovell Jewels*, Oxford, 1948.

LEEDS, E. T., *Early Anglo-Saxon Art and Archaeology*, Oxford, 1936.

LEVISON, W., *England and the Continent in the Eighth Century*, Oxford, 1946.

LOWE, E. A., *Codices Latini Antiquiores*, vol II, Oxford, 1935.

LOYN, H. R., *Anglo-Saxon England and the Norman Conquest*, London, 1962.

MEANEY, A., *A Gazetteer of Early Anglo-Saxon Burial Sites*, London, 1964.

MYRES, J. N. L., *Anglo-Saxon Pottery and the Settlement of England*, Oxford, 1969.

OMAN, C., *A History of the Art of War in the Middle Ages* (2nd ed.), London, 1924.

PETERSEN, J., *De Norske Vikingesverd*, Kristiania, 1919.

RICKERT, M., *Painting in Britain, The Middle Ages*, London, 1954.

ROBERTSON, A. J., *Anglo-Saxon Charters* (2nd ed.), Cambridge, 1956.

SALIN, B., *Die altgermanische Thierornamentik* (2nd ed.), Stockholm, 1935.

SINGER, C., HOLMYARD, E. J., HALL, A. R. and WILLIAMS, T. I., *A History of Technology*, Vol. II, Oxford, 1956.

STENTON, F. M., *Anglo-Saxon England*, Oxford, 1943.

STENTON, F. M. *The Bayeux Tapestry*, London 1957.

STONE, L., *Sculpture in Britain; the Middle Ages*, London, 1955.

TALBOT RICE, D., *English Art 871–1100*, Oxford, 1952.

TAYLOR, H. M. and J., *Anglo-Saxon Architecture*, Cambridge, 1965.

TISCHLER, F., 'Der Stand der Sachsenforschung, archäologisch gesehen', *Bericht der Römisch-Germanischen Kommission*, 35, 1954.

WHEELER, R. E. M., *London and the Vikings*, London, 1927.

WHEELER, R. E. M., *London and the Saxons*, London, 1935.

WHITELOCK, D., *The Beginnings of English Society*, London, 1952.

WHITELOCK, D., *English Historical Documents*, London, 1955.

WILSON, D. M., *Anglo-Saxon Ornamental Metalwork 700–1100 in the British Museum*, London, 1964.

WILSON, D. M. and KLINDT-JENSEN, O., *Viking Art*, London, 1966.

WORMALD, F., *English Drawings of the Tenth and Eleventh Centuries*, London, 1952.

WORMALD, F., *The Benedictional of St Ethelwold*, London, 1959.

ZIMMERMANN, E. H., *Vorkarolingische Miniaturen*, Berlin, 1916.

Sources of Illustrations

The line illustrations, with the exception of Fig. 7, which is taken from Stephens', *Runic Monuments*, are either original drawings, or re-drawn from published illustrations, by Mrs Eva Wilson.

The majority of the photographs from which the plates are made were taken by Mr G. Ashburner of the Colour Centre. Other sources are as follows: Ashmolean Museum, Pl. 22; Bibliothèque Nationale, Paris, Pl. 50; British Museum, Pls. 1, 2, 17, 18, 26, 27, 30, 31, 32, 36, 37, 39, 45, 49, 52, 63, 69, 70, 71, 79; Cambridge University Museum of Archaeology and Ethnology, Pl. 34; Guildhall Museum, London, Pl. 74; Mrs G. Keiller, Pl. 43; The Laurentian Library, Florence, Pl. 47; David Leigh, Pl. 75; M. Paul Lemare, Pl. 16; Lensmen, Dublin, Pl. 46; National Buildings Record, Pl. 13; Österreichische Lichtbildstelle, Pl. 61; Royal Commission on Historical Monuments (England), Pls. 66, 73; Mr E. Smith, Pls. 12, 15; Dr F. Stoedtner, Pl. 48; Victoria and Albert Museum, London, Pl. 51; Warburg Institute, Pl. 53; Yorkshire Museum, Pl. 67; and the author, Pls. 14, 25, 72, 76, 77.

Notes on the Plates

In the light of the remarks in the introduction, it should be emphasized that the dates given in these notes are intended only as a general indication for the convenience of the reader.

1. One of a pair of curved jewelled clasps from the Sutton Hoo ship burial. A pin with an animal-head top, attached by a chain to the clasp, can be withdrawn to break the clasp into two parts. The clasp was sewn on to a cloth base by means of loops on the underside. The surface is decorated with garnets and mosaic glass (cf. Fig. 3). Early seventh century. Length: 12.4 cm. London, British Museum.

2. Gold mounts, some inlaid with garnets, from the hilt of the sword from the Sutton Hoo ship burial. The two domed circular mounts were attached to the scabbard and the truncated pyramidal mounts came, presumably, from the sword belt. Late sixth or early seventh century. Length of the pommel: 6.5 cm. London, British Museum.

3. Two of a suite of ten shallow silver bowls, of provincial Byzantine origin, from the Sutton Hoo ship burial. Late sixth or early seventh century. Diameter of each: approx. 20 cm. London, British Museum.

4. Small jewelled buckle from the Sutton Hoo ship burial: of gold, it is inlaid with garnets. Late sixth or early seventh century. Length: 4.5 cm. London, British Museum.

5. Gold strap distributor, set with garnets, from the Sutton Hoo ship burial. The upper portion swivels laterally through 90° from the position shown in the photograph. The central element is hinged. Straps were attached by the gold rivets at the terminals. Late sixth or early seventh century. Length: 5.3 cm. London, British Museum.

6. Gold buckle, decorated with garnets, from the Sutton Hoo ship burial. This buckle belongs to the same suite of mounts as the

adjacent strap distributor. Late sixth or early seventh century. Length: 7.7 cm. London, British Museum.

7. The great buckle from the Sutton Hoo ship burial, decorated with nielloed, interlaced snakes and other animal ornament (see Fig. 32). Early seventh century. Length: 13.2 cm. London, British Museum.

8. Helmet from the Sutton Hoo ship burial. The helmet, which was probably made in Sweden in the sixth century, consists of an iron cap covered with impressed bronze sheets and further embellished with silver and bronze gilt additions. Notice the garnets on the eyebrows. The helmet has been much restored. Height: approx. 31.8 cm. London, British Museum.

9. Jewelled purse-lid from the Sutton Hoo ship burial. The white background is modern; the plaques would originally have been set in leather or ivory. The cells contain garnets and fragments of mosaic glass. The purse contained 37 gold coins of Merovingian France, 3 blank coins and two ingots. Early seventh century. 18.8 cm. London, British Museum.

10. Terminal of the large whetstone (sceptre?) from the Sutton Hoo ship burial. The bronze cage is surmounted by a saucer-shaped plate and covers a red-painted terminal knob. Late sixth or early seventh century. Length of portion illustrated: approx. 13.0 cm. London, British Museum.

11. Mount from the inside of the largest hanging-bowl from the Sutton Hoo ship burial, showing a bronze fish standing on a pillar erected in the centre of an enamelled disc. Late sixth or early seventh century. Length of the fish: 9.3 cm. London, British Museum.

12. The tower of the parish church at Earls Barton, Northamptonshire. It is one of the finest surviving pieces of Anglo-Saxon architecture in this country. The topmost courses and the battlements of the tower are modern, but the greater portion of the tower is of tenth century date. The basic rubble work is plastered and enriched by pilaster strips, arcading and other sculptural details. Height of tower with modern additions: nearly 21 m.

13. Internal view of the church at Escomb, Co. Durham, one of the most complete Anglo-Saxon churches. The round-headed, narrow chancel arch, with its radial voussoirs, is to be noted, as are the round-headed windows and square-topped door. It may be dated to the late seventh century. Internal width of the nave: approx. 4.4 m.

14. The tenth-century apse of the parish church of All Saints at Wing, Buckinghamshire. The majority of the fabric of the Anglo-Saxon church survives, but the south aisle and the tower of the church,

seen in this illustration, are of fourteenth- and fifteenth-century date respectively. External length of the apse: 7 m.

15. The church of St Lawrence at Bradford-on-Avon, Wiltshire. Built by Aldhelm in the late seventh or early eighth century, restored with additions in the tenth century (when the angel illustrated in Pl. 73 was added) and, having been used for domestic purposes, it was rediscovered in 1858 and carefully restored. External length: approx. 14.6 m.

16. Oak portable altar with porphyry centre and a parcel-gilt silver binding. At the top is a crucifixion, at the bottom an *Agnus Dei*. Also portrayed are the evangelist symbols, archangels, Mary and St John. Tenth century. Length: 26.4 cm. Paris, Musée de Cluny.

17. Silver chalice from the Trewhiddle hoard (see Pl. 63). One of two surviving Anglo-Saxon chalices; the inside was originally gilded. The chalice has been reconstructed. Ninth century. Height: 12 cm. London, British Museum.

18. Two plates from a tenth-century house-shaped shrine. They are of silver, inlaid with niello, the upper plate being decorated with animal ornament (see Fig. 38). Length of rectangular mount: 12.4 cm. London, British Museum.

19. A selection of Anglo-Saxon silver pennies of various periods; both the obverse and the reverse of each coin are shown. Left to right: Offa, *c.* 785; Alfred, *c.* 886; Edward the Elder, *c.* 920; Edward the Elder, *c.* 920; Sihtric the One-Eyed, *c.* 923; Anlaf Guthfrithson, *c.* 940; Edward the Martyr, *c.* 975; Ethelred II, summer of 1009; Ethelred II, *c.* 1010; Ethelred II, *c.* 1010; Cnut, *c.* 1025; Edward the Confessor, autumn of 1065. London, British Museum.

20. Group of cruciform brooches. Left to right: Green Bank, Co. Durham; West Stow Heath, Suffolk; Barrington, Cambridgeshire; Barrington, Cambridgeshire. Sixth century. Length of largest example: 15 cm. Oxford, Ashmolean Museum.

21. Group of saucer brooches. Left to right: Cassington, Oxfordshire; Wheatley, Oxfordshire; Brighthampton, Oxfordshire; Fairford, Gloucestershire; Brighthampton; Fairford. Diameter of largest example: 8.3 cm. Oxford, Ashmolean Museum.

22. The Abingdon sword. The hilt of this sword, as illustrated, has nielloed silver plates inlaid into the pommel and the guard. From New Cut Mill, Abingdon, Berkshire. Length of guard: 12 cm. Ninth century. Oxford, Ashmolean Museum.

23. Hilt of a sword found in the bank of the River Witham, near Lincoln. The silver plates, with which it is decorated, are engraved with degenerate animal ornament and inlaid with niello. Ninth

century. Length of pommel: 6.8 cm. Sheffield, City Museum.

24. The Fetter Lane sword pommel. Found in Fetter Lane, London, it is executed in carved parcel-gilt silver, inlaid with niello. The design depicts a series of whirling snakes. Ninth century. Length: 9.5 cm. London, British Museum.

25. Fragment of the leather scabbard of a *scramasax* from Hexham, Northumberland, decorated with an interlaced ribbon pattern. Length: 11.2 cm. London, British Museum.

26. *Scramasax* found at Sittingbourne, Kent. Inlaid with copper, silver, niello and bronze, it records the name of the maker, BIORK-TELM, and the owner, SGEBEREHT. Tenth century. Length: 32.3 cm. London, British Museum.

27. *Scramasax* with silver pommel and guard; found with the hanging-bowl, illustrated in Pl. 45, and a spearhead in a grave at Winchester. Seventh century. Length: 40.5 cm. London, British Museum.

28. The boar from the Benty Grange helmet, depicted in Pl. 29. Length: 9.5 cm. Sheffield, City Museum.

29. The framework of the seventh-century helmet found at Benty Grange, Derbyshire. The cap was originally made up of horn plates attached by means of the iron bands which are all that survives. The nosepiece, bottom left, bears an inlaid silver cross. Sheffield, City Museum.

30. Bronze buckle from Worms, Germany, showing the common provincial Roman chip-carved ornament. Fourth–fifth century. Length: 7 cm. London, British Museum.

31. Bronze chip-carved buckle and counter-plate of provincial Roman type from Kent (?). Fourth–fifth century. Length: 11.4 cm. London, British Museum.

32. Bronze chip-carved buckle of provincial Roman type from Smithfield, London. Fourth–fifth century. Length: 8.2 cm. London, British Museum.

33. Gold and garnet necklace from a woman's grave at Desborough, Northamptonshire. Seventh century. Length of central cross: 2.5 cm. London, British Museum.

34. Silver-gilt, chip-carved, equal-armed brooch from Haslingfield, Cambridgeshire. The brooch might have been made on the Continent or by one of the earliest Anglo-Saxon settlers in this country. Fifth century. Length: 10 cm. Cambridge, University Museum of Archaeology and Ethnology.

35. The Kingston Brooch. The richest piece of Anglo-Saxon jewellery found outside the Sutton Hoo grave, from Kingston Down,

grave 205, Kent. The surface is decorated with gold filigree ornament, cuttle-fish shell, garnets and blue stone. The pressed foil backing to the garnets can be clearly seen in the empty cells. Seventh century. Diameter: 8.4 cm. Liverpool, City Museum.

36. Jewelled disc brooch of Kentish type from Breach Down, Kent. The brooch is of silver-gilt and the zig-zag border pattern is inlaid with niello. Cast cells are inlaid with garnets. Sixth century. Diameter: 3.8 cm. London, British Museum.

37. Jewelled disc brooch of Kentish type from Faversham, Kent. Sixth century. Diameter: 4 cm. London, British Museum.

38. Gold and garnet pendant from Faversham, Kent. The flat back-plate is decorated with filigree wire, the three whirling animal-heads in the centre being executed in cloisonné garnets. The eyes of the animals are set *en cabochon*. Seventh century. Diameter: 11.4 cm. London, British Museum.

39. Gold and garnet buckle-plate, from Wynaldum, Friesland, Holland, built up on a silver back-plate. In the upper panel are a pair of tortuous backward-looking quadrupeds. Seventh century. Length: 9.2 cm. Leeuwarden (Holland), Fries Museum.

40. Pectoral cross of St Cuthbert. This cross was found in the tomb of St Cuthbert in Durham Cathedral. It was presumably placed in the coffin on the death of St Cuthbert in 687. The lower arm has been damaged and repaired in antiquity. Of gold, shell and garnet, it is one of the latest pieces of garnet jewellery known from an Anglo-Saxon context. Seventh century. Breadth: 6 cm. Durham, Cathedral Library.

41. The Ixworth cross. Found in a grave at Stanton, Ixworth, Suffolk, it is of gold inlaid with thick garnets. Seventh century. Breadth: 3.8 cm. Oxford, Ashmolean Museum.

42. The Wilton cross. This gold and garnet jewelled pendant, found at Wilton, Norfolk, contains a coin of Heraclius (610–41), the Byzantine Emperor. Perhaps from the Sutton Hoo workshop. Seventh century. Height: 4.9 cm. London, British Museum.

43. Enamelled bronze mounts from a hanging-bowl found at Middleton by Youlgrave, Derbyshire. Sixth–seventh century. Diameter of disc: 5.2 cm. Sheffield, City Museum.

44. Two gold clasps, ornamented with filigree techniques, and a gold and garnet buckle, from a rich seventh-century barrow at Taplow, Buckinghamshire. Length of buckle: 10.2 cm. London, British Museum.

45. Hanging-bowl, found with a spearhead and the *scramasax* illustrated in Pl. 27, in a grave at Winchester. The escutcheon is inlaid

with red enamel. Seventh century. Diameter at rim: 28.2 cm. London, British Museum.

46. The Book of Durrow (fol. 21b). Portrait of the Evangelist Matthew. The body of the Evangelist is an abstract expression of the naturalism of the Mediterranean model from which it is derived. The colours of the page are red, yellow and green. Second half of the seventh century. Length of page: 24.3 cm. Dublin, Library of Trinity College.

47. Codex Amiatinus. This page (the Ezra folio) has in the past been described as Italian. Recent research, however, suggests most strongly that it is Anglo-Saxon and it illustrates well the classicism of a certain type of seventh-century Anglo-Saxon manuscript art. Length of page: 49 cm. Florence, Biblioteca Laurentiana.

48. The Lindisfarne Gospels (fol. 47b). One of the great carpet pages, illuminated with interlaced animals and birds. Painted just before the year 700. Length: 34.5 cm. London, British Museum.

49. The Lindisfarne Gospels (fol. 25b). Page portraying the Evangelist John, surmounted by his symbol. Painted just before the year 700. Length: 34.5 cm. London, British Museum.

50. Echternach Gospels (fol. 18b). Symbol of the Evangelist Matthew, painted in Northumbria (possibly in the Lindisfarne *scriptorium*) about the year 700. Length: 26.2 cm. Paris, Bibliothèque Nationale.

51. St Chad Gospels (p. 142). Portrait of the Evangelist Mark, surmounted by his symbol the lion. Painted in Northumbria in the early eighth century. Length: 24.5 cm. Lichfield, Cathedral Library.

52. Page of canon tables from the M.S. Royal 1.E.VI (fol. 4a) in the British Museum. In the borders, which surround these tables of concordance, are ornaments which can be compared to that on eighth- and ninth-century metalwork. Early ninth century. Length: 47 cm. London, British Museum.

53. The Ruthwell cross. Two views, showing on one face various Christian scenes and on the side a typical Northumbrian inhabited vine-scroll. Ruthwell, Dumfries.

54. Panel from St Cuthbert's coffin. Upper half of the figure of Christ carved on the lid of the coffin reliquary. His right hand is raised in blessing and He carries a book in His left hand. Late seventh century. Durham, Cathedral Library.

55. The Witham pins (cf. Fig. 33). Set of three, linked, circular, gilt-bronze pins found in the river Witham, near Fiskerton, Lincolnshire. The ornament is executed in the chip-carved technique and the

eyes of the animals are inlaid with blue glass. Eighth century. Length of central pin: 12 cm. London, British Museum.

56. The Franks Casket. Whalebone ivory casket, of Northumbrian workmanship, carved with scenes from a universal history. The scenes are surrounded by inscriptions in runes. Early eighth century. Length: 22.3 cm. London, British Museum.

57. The Alfred Jewel. Made of gold with a cloisonné enamel portrait set under crystal. This jewel was found at Newton Park, Somerset in 1693. Round the edge of the upper portion is an inscription which, when translated, reads, *Alfred ordered me to be made*. This presumably refers to King Alfred (871–99). Length: 7.4 cm. Oxford, Ashmolean Museum.

58. Back of the Alfred Jewel, showing the engraved foliate pattern on the gold back-plate.

59. The Minster Lovell jewel. Found at Minster Lovell, Oxfordshire. Constructed in the same manner as the Alfred Jewel (Pl. 57), it is perhaps slightly later in date (tenth century?). Length: 3.2 cm. Oxford, Ashmolean Museum.

60. The Dowgate Hill brooch. Found in Dowgate Hill, London, it is of gold filigree and enamel. Its close resemblance to the Alfred Jewel (Pl. 57) is very striking. Ninth–tenth century. Diameter: 3.3 cm. London, British Museum.

61. The Tassilo Chalice. Gilt-bronze vessel inscribed with the name of Tassilo III, Duke of Bavaria 748–88, and given by him to the monastery of Kremsmünster, which was founded in 777. Height: 26.7 cm. Kremsmünster Monastery, Austria.

62. The Kirkoswald brooch. This filigree silver trefoil brooch, set with garnets (of which only one survives), was found at Kirkoswald, Cumberland, with coins which date its deposition to between 850 and 860. Eighth–ninth century. Length: 8.9 cm. London, British Museum.

63. Material from the Trewhiddle hoard (see also Pl. 17 and Fig. 35). Found at Trewhiddle, near St Austell, Cornwall, with coins which date its deposition to *c.* 875. The objects shown include strap ends, strap slides, pin and curved drinking-horn mounts. Many of the objects are decorated with animal ornament in the 'Trewhiddle style'. London, British Museum.

64. The Strickland brooch. Of silver, inlaid with gold plates and niello, it is so called after Sir William Strickland who is presumed to have acquired it in the early nineteenth century. Ninth century. Diameter: 11 cm. London, British Museum.

65. The Fuller brooch. A silver disc brooch inlaid with niello and

portraying, in the central panels, the five senses, taste, smell, hearing, touch and sight. Ninth century. Diameter: 11.2 cm. London, British Museum.

66. Head of a carved stone cross from Cropthorne, Worcestershire. Ninth century. Cropthorne Parish Church.

67. Bone trial-piece from Station Road, York. Showing animals (similar in style to those on objects from the Trewhiddle hoard) being tried out on a piece of discarded bone. Ninth century. Length: 11 cm. York, Yorkshire Museum.

68. Two portions of the stole of St Cuthbert, executed at Winchester (?) between 909 and 916 and probably presented to the shrine of St Cuthbert by King Æthelstan in 934. Left, St Peter; right, Jonah. Length of portion illustrated: approx. 18 cm. Durham, Cathedral Library.

69. Page (fol. 5b) from the Benedictional of St Æthelwold, illustrating the Annunciation. This page illustrates the height of Winchester lavishness. Made for, or at the order of, Æthelwold, Bishop of Winchester 971–84. Length: 19 cm. London, British Museum.

70. Page (fol. 2b) from the Charter of the New Minster at Winchester. King Edgar is seen offering the charter to Christ, who sits in a mandorla. The page must have been painted in the early eleventh century. Length: 20.5 cm. London, British Museum.

71. Detail of fol. 51b of a psalter (British Museum MS., Harley 603). Executed in a variety of coloured inks; the colours used in the portion illustrated (the heading of Psalm 103) are red, black, blue and brown. Date: *c.* 1000. Height of the portion illustrated: approx. 29.2 cm. London, British Museum.

72. Fragments of Anglo-Saxon carved stone crosses and tombstones in the porch of Bakewell Church, Derbyshire. The fragments illustrate different styles of Anglo-Saxon interlace ornament.

73. Angel, carved in stone, from the church of St Lawrence at Bradford-on-Avon (see Pl. 15). One of the finest pieces of late Saxon stone sculpture, it can be compared with angels depicted in Pls. 70 and 75. Tenth century. Length: about 150 cm. Royal Commission on Historical Monuments (England).

74. Tombstone from St Paul's churchyard, London, executed in the Ringerike Style. The surface was originally painted with two or three colours and the body of the animal was speckled with white dots. Tenth–eleventh century. Length: 61 cm. London, the Guildhall Museum.

75. Ivory panel, from Winchester, carved in the Winchester style; an expression in ivory of the figural style which can be seen in Pls.

70 and 73. Tenth century. Height approx. 7.6 cm. Winchester, City Museum.

76–77. Two sides of a comb of walrus ivory, showing on one face an interlaced animal inspired by Viking art and on the other an Anglo-Saxon animal which can be compared with those on the censer cover illustrated in Pl. 79. Early eleventh century. Height 5.2 cm. London, British Museum.

78. The Sutton brooch. Found at Sutton, Isle of Ely, in 1694 with coins of William I. The brooch is decorated with Ringerike Style ornament. On the back of the brooch is inscribed a curse in Anglo-Saxon. Tenth–eleventh century. Diameter: 15 cm. London, British Museum.

79. Bronze censer cover, from Canterbury, in the form of a building: the lower borders and the hips of the animals are inlaid with nielloed silver plates. Tenth–eleventh century. Height: 12 cm. London, British Museum.

Index

Abingdon, 33, 34, 110, 113, 165
Acca, St, Bishop, 56–7
ad Gefrin, Yeavering, 15, 64
adzes, 78
Ælfflaed, Queen, 57
Ælfric, *Colloquy*, 88
Æthelbald, King, 31
Æthelbert, King, 38, 48
Æthelfrith, King, 64
Æthelhere, King, 46–7
Æthelred II, King, 22, 85, 165
Æthelstan, King, 32, 58, 95, 170
Æthelswith, Queen, 19, 62
Æthilwald, Bishop, 19
Æthelwold, St, 32, 151 (*see* also Benedictional of)
Æthelwulf, King, 19
Æthelwynn, Lady, 58
Ætheric, 128
Agathias, 124–5
Agriculture, 16, 23, 63–80
Alcester, 60
Alcuin, 82, 92
Aldhelm, 93, 165
Alfred, King, 25, 31, 65, 84, 85, 92, 142, 147, 151, 165, 169
Alfred Jewel, 19, 142–3, 169
Almgren, Professor B., 18
Altars, 49, 55, 57
portable, 56–7, 59, 157, 165
amber, 87, 97
Anastasius, Emperor, 41

Angles, 26, 27, 34, 36–40
Anglo-Saxon Chronicle, 31, 48, 82, 85, 92, 123
angons, 41, 124–5
animal ornament, 95, 134, 164, 165, 170
Anlaf Guthfrithson, 165
Anna, King, 46–7
Arabs, 87
architecture, 48–55
arrows, 121, 123–4
art, 61, 131–58
Arthur, King, 29, 85
Ashford, 106
Ashlar, 51
Asser, 128
Æthelstan, Atheling, 18
Atkinson, Professor, R. J. C., 109, 117
auger, 77, 78
Augustine, St, 48–9, 50, 82
mission of, 30, 48, 49, 139
monastery of, 51
aurochs, 41
axes, 41, 77, 78, 121–2

Bakewell Church, Derbs., 170
Baldwin-Brown, Professor G., 20, 108, 123
Barrington, 165
Barton, K., 71
Bateman, T., 109
battle, tactics of, 126–30

Bayeux Tapestry, 76, 77, 89, 90, 105, 118, 121, 123, 124, 125, 126

beads, 97

Beddington, 125

Bede, 15, 24, 26, 30, 37, 42, 45, 64, 84, 145

Beeston Tor, 19

Benedict Biscop, 52, 53, 61, 145

Benedictional of Robert of Jumièges, 152

Benedictional of St Æthelwold, 152–3, 170

Benty Grange, 62, 122, 125, 138, 166

Beowulf, 35–6, 109, 110, 122

Berkhamsted, 124

Bernicia, 15, 28, 29, 64

Bertha, Queen, 48, 49

Beverley, 61

Bewcastle, 54, 149

Biddle, Mr, 24

Bifrons, 108, 123, 125

bill-hooks, 76, 80

Biorktelm, 115, 166

Birka, Sweden, 87

Bishofshofen, Austria, 60

Blackwater, river, 126, 127

Blair, H., 37

Blunt, C. E., 21

Blythburgh, 46

boars, 122, 166

boats, 91–2

bones, animal, 73, 77

bowls, 41, 42, 55, 89, 137–8, 144, 146, 163, 166, 167

bows, 121, 123–4

Bradford-on-Avon, 51, 52, 154, 165, 170

Breach Down, 167

Breedon-on-the-Hill, 52

Brighthampton, 109, 165

Bristol, 154

brooches, 17, 18, 33, 34, 36, 37, 39, 48, 61, 70, 93, 94, 95–7, 132, 136–7, 140, 141, 143, 156, 157, 165, 166, 167, 169, 171

long brooches, 22

Brooks, Mr, 84

Broomfield, 40

Brown, Professor J., 146

Bruce-Mitford, R. L. S., 137

Brushfield, 109

Byrhtnoth, 126–8

buckets, 41, 55

Buckden, 73, 98

Buckelurnen, 101, 102

buckles, 23, 33, 43, 70, 98, 132–3, 134, 135, 136, 137, 163, 166, 167

burial customs, 33–6, 48

Burwell, 108

Caenby, 115

Caister-by-Norwich, 26

Caister-on-Sea, 26

Cambridge, 39, 99

Camelot, 85

Canterbury, 36, 49, 50, 51, 53, 60, 81–2, 84, 146, 153, 156, 157

Archbishop of, 86

Canterbury Psalter, 146

Canute, King, 22, 32

Carlisle, 84

Carolingian manuscripts, 112, 146

Cassington, 69, 165

cattle, 77–80

Celtic art, 41, 42, 45, 95, 137–8, 146

cemeteries, 23, 24, 33–5, 36, 37, 40, 65, 68, 70, 82, 99, 105

censers, 55, 60, 157, 171

Cedlfrith, Abbot, 145

Cenwulf, 31

cereals, 73, 77
Chad, St, Gospels of, 146, 168
chalices, 48, 55, 58–9, 165, 169
chancels, 49, 50, 53
Charibert, King of Franks, 48
Charlemagne, 92
chateláine, 34, 39, 97
Cheddar, 24, 64, 65–6, 72, 73, 75
Cheshire, 32
Chessel Down, 109, 111, 120, 123
Chester, 18, 104
Chester-le Street, 49
Christ Church, monastery of, 53
Childeric, King of Franks, 40, 137
chip-carving, 133–6, 166
Chichester, 89
Christianity, 15, 17, 34, 48–9, 56, 61
    traces of, 61–2
    effect of, on art, 139
chronology, 17–22
churches, 17, 24, 48–53, 67, 68
church plate, 61, 156
civil service established by Æthelstan, 32
clasps, 39, 43–4, 136, 144, 163, 167
cloisonné jewellery, 136–8, 167, 169
cloth, 77, 87–9
Cluny Altar, 57
Cnut, King, 85, 165
Codex Amiatinus, 145, 168
Codex Aureus (Stockholm), 146
coins, 17, 18, 21, 22, 32, 46, 62, 86–7, 157, 165, 167
Colchester, 85
Colloquy, Ælfric, 88
Cologne, Germany, 60
combs, 16, 34, 56, 57, 97–8, 156, 171
Coptic bowls, 21
coracles, 92

Cornwall, 21, 32
Cotton Tiberius, *C. VI* (MS.) 114
Cowlow, 40
cowrie shells, 21, 40, 89
Cramp, Miss R., 24
cremation, 33–5, 36
Crondall, 19, 86
Cropthorne, 150, 170
crosses, 48, 54, 62
    altar, 60
    of Rupert, 60
    pectoral, 56, 139, 162
    stone, 17, 24, 54–5, 170
    Ixworth, 167
    Bewcastle, 149
    Middleton, 155
    Reculver, 61, 149
    Ruthwell, 148–9, 150, 168
    Wilton, 167
    Cropthorne, 150, 170
Crowfoot, Mrs G., 23
Croydon, 106
croziers, 60
Crundale Down, 135
Cuerdale, 19
Cumberland, sword hilts in, 110
Cunliffe, Professor B., 67–8, 75
cups, 41, 55
Cura Pastoralis, Gregory, 30, 147
Cuthbert, St, life of (MS.), 152
Cuthbert, St, relics of, 19, 21, 55–8, 59, 95, 139, 150, 151–2, 167, 168, 170

Davidson, B., 23, 66, 83
Deben, River, 40
Deira, 28, 29
dendrochronology, 17, 20
Desborough, 56, 97, 166
diet, 16, 20, 23, 34, 73, 80
dishes, 41, 55, 56 (*see also* church plate)

dogs, 87, 88
Dolley, R. H. M., 21, 22
Dolven, Norway, 113
Domesday Book, 68, 77, 83
Doon Hill, 65
Dorchester, 84
Dorchester-on-Thames, 82
Dowgate Hill, 143, 169
Drinking Horns, 41, 58, 105, 106, 134–6
Dream of the Rood, The, 149
dress, 16, 23, 92–8
Durham, 55, 152, 167
Dunstan, St, 58, 151, 152
Durrow, Book of, 144–6, 168

Eadfrith, Bishop, 145
Earls Barton, 51, 53, 67, 164
ear rings, 98
East Anglia, 30, 44, 46, 102, 104, 136, 137
Ecclesiastical History, Bede, 64
Ecgric, 46–7
Echternach Gospels, 145–6, 148, 168
Edda, Poetic, 111
Eddington, Battle of, 31
Edgar, King, 22, 32, 82, 87, 151, 153, 170
Edward the Confessor, King, 32, 33, 165
   cross of, 19
Edward the Elder, King, 32, 62, 165
Edward the Martyr, 165
Edwin, King, 15, 30, 45, 48, 49, 64
Edwy, King, 65
Egbert, King, 31
Eichstatt, 54
Eifel, Germany, 77
Einhard, 92–3

Ely, 55, 126
embroidery, 151–2
England, establishment of, 29–31
   colonization and conquest of, 27–9, 31
   conversion to Christianity, 48–50
Eorpwald, 46–7
Escomb, 53, 164
Essex, 29, 30, 38
Evans, Sir John, 13
Exeter, 113
Eynsham, 69

Fairford, 165
farms, 63, 71
Farne Island, 55
Faversham, 105, 106, 167
Fife, 89
fish-hooks, 81
Fleam Dike, 111
Fletcher, Sir Eric, 23, 49
Fowler, Mr P., 73
Fox, Sir Cyril, 23
Franks Casket, 93, 122, 123, 150, 169
Franks, Sir Augustus, 150
Frere, Professor S. S., 36
Frilford, 34
Frisians, 27, 28, 87
Frithestan, Bishop, 57
Fuller brooch, 141, 169
Fusion Style, 136
Fyfield Down, 73

Gandersheim Casket, 59, 61, 138
Garannes, Ireland, 42
garnet, 23, 38, 43, 44, 56, 89, 97, 122, 136, 163–71, *passim*
Gaul, 52, 69, 80
Geats, 35
Germanus, 81
Gilton, sword hilt, in 110

girdles, 57–8
glass, 105–7
Glastonbury, 49, 105
goats, 77
Godescalc, Evangeliar, 146
Godule, S., Brussels, 60
Gokstad, Norway, 115
Gordon, Profesor E. U., 129
Gospel Book, 56, 145
Gravesend, 19
Green Bank, 165
Greensted, 49
Gregory, *Cora Pastoralis*, 30, 147
Gregory, Pope, 48
Gregory of Tours, 113
Grierson, Dr P., 21, 46
Grimes, Professor, W. F., 24
Gronneberg, Norway, 113
graves, 33–5, 55, 70, 82, 91, 100
    luxury goods found in, 16, 21,
    22, 27, 34–6, 40, 48, 54, 76,
    94–6, 102, 105, 108, 118
    skeletons found in, 23

hair, care of, 93–4
Haithabu, 87
Halton, 155
Hamwih, 84
Harden, Dr O. B., 105
Harold, King, 33
harp, 41
harrow, 77
Harthacnut, King, 32
Hartlepool, 54
Haslingfield, 133, 166
Hastings, Battle of, 122
Hatfield, 77
Hawkes, Mrs S. E. C., 94, 132
Hedeby, Germany, 124
helmets, 121, 122–3, 164
    Benty Grange, 62, 122, 123,
    125, 138, 166

Hengist, 25, 27
Henry, Dr F., 42
Henry of Huntingdon, 124
Heraclius, 167
Hereford, 84
Hexham, 19, 58, 109, 166
High Down, 125
Hillier, Mr, 123
hoards, 18, 21, 22
Hodgkin, Dr R. H., 38
Holborough, 103
Holland, 26, 27
Holywell Row, 108
Hon, Norway, 19
Hope-Taylor, Dr B., 15, 23, 24,
    49, 64–5, 75
Horsa, 25, 27
horses, 80, 88
Hough-on-the-Hill, 45, 138
Houghton-on the-Hill, 101
houses, 72–3
Howletts, 121
Hoxne, 114
Humber, river, 26, 30
Hurbuck, 76, 77, 78

Ibn Khordadbeh, 87
Icklingham, long-brooches, 96
Ingelosa, Sweden, 19
Illington, 99, 101
Inglesham, 154
inhumation, 33–5
invasions, the Anglo-Saxon, 29–33
Ipswich, 99, 102, 103
Ixworth, 56, 167
ivory, 43, 57, 60, 61, 62, 88, 138,
    143
    African, 21
    plaque, Winchester, 154–5, 170

Jackson, E. D. C., 23
Janes, Mrs, 71

Jarrow, 42, 51, 52, 61
Jellinge, Style, 155, 157
Jessup, R., 23
jewellery, 16, 23, 38–40, 43, 44, 47, 48, 56, 86, 92–8, 132–7
Jews, 87–8
Junius Psalter, 152
Jutarum Natio, Bede, 38
Jutes, 26, 27, 28, 36–40
Jutland, 27, 38

Keller, Miss M. L., 123
Kells, crozier, 141, 143
Kempston, 105
Kendrick, Sir Thomas, 45, 54, 131, 134, 147, 149, 154
Kent, 26, 28, 38, 81, 132–3, 136, 137, 166
Kent, Dr J. P. C., 46
kiln sites, 16, 83, 98–100, 104, 105–7
Kingston, 108, 137, 166
Kirkoswald, 19, 139–40
Kitzinger, Professor E., 150
knives, 34, 98
knives, 34, 98 (*see also scramas-axes*)
draw-, 81
Knocker, Group Capt. G, 23, 83
Kremsmünster, Austria, monastery of, 59, 141, 169

Lackford, 99, 101
lacti, 26, 69, 70, 82 (*see also* mercenaries)
Laking, Sir Guy, 123
Langres, France, 145
Lark, river, 110, 138
Leeds, E. T., 20, 36, 98
leet, 77
Leland, 61
Lethbridge, T. C., 20

Lincoln, 84, 85
Lindisfarne, 31, 49
Lindisfarne Gospels, 138, 141, 145–7, 148, 150, 168
Lindsey, 29, 30
Linford, 71
Linton, 117
Little Wilbrahan, 99
liturgical equipment, 17, 42
Liudhard, Bishop, 48
Lombardy, 88
London, 30, 71, 82, 84, 85, 87, 89, 91
London:
   All Hallows, 155
   Fetter Lane, 112, 141, 166
   London Bridge, 60
   St Paul's churchyard, 61, 156, 170
   Smithfield, 166
   Savoy Palace, 102
Long Wittenham, 34, 134
Loyn, Professor H. R., 85
Lydd, 23
Lydford, 83, 84
lyre, 41

Maastricht, Holland, 60
mail, 125–6
Maldon, Battle of, 126–30
maniple, 57–8, 95, 151
mantle, 92, 97
Mann, Sir James, 126
manuscript art, 143–7, 152–4
Martin, St, church of, 49
Maxey, 71
meat preserving, 80
Melbourn, 34, 116
Memlin, 64
mercenaries, 27, 29, 37 (*see also laeti*)
merchants, 87–9

Mercia, 24, 26, 29, 30–1, 32, 38, 39, 47
metalwork, 139–143, 156–8
Middlesex, 29
Middleton, 155
Middleton Moor, 138
mills, 77
Minster Lovell, 143, 169
minting, 21, 82, 86–7
monasteries, 46, 61, 102
  Bede's, 24, 42
  Jarrow, 145
  Kremünster, Austria, 59
  St Augustine's, 51
Monkwearmouth, 24, 51, 52, 53, 61, 145
Montelius, Oscar, 13, 14, 17
moot, 15, 49
Morley, St Peter, 18
Mortain Casket, 61
Mucking, 16, 34, 69, 70–1, 132–3, 134
Myres, Dr J. N. L., 27, 37, 70–1, 99, 101

Naegling, 109
necklaces, 97, 166
Nelson, Dr, 61
New Minster, Winchester, Charter of, 153, 154, 170
  register of, 60
Newton Park, 142, 169
niello, 43, 57, 60, 112, 136, 140, 141, 147, 164, 165, 166, 167, 169, 171
Norfolk, 83
Normandy, Duke of, 32
Normans, 32–3
North Elmham, 83
Northey, Island of, 126
Northumbria, 26, 29, 30, 31, 32, 37, 42, 45, 48, 61, 64, 65, 168

Norwich, 85
Nydam, Jutland, 40

Oberflacht, Germany, 118, 120, 123
Offa, King, 20, 25, 31, 81, 86, 108, 165
Offa's Dyke, 24
Old Windsor, 24, 66, 77
Ofton, 114
opus anglicanum, 151
orbs, 115–18
Oswald, King, 30, 32
Oswald, St, 54, 151
Oswiu, King, 30
Oswy, King, 64
Ouse, river, Thetford, 82
Oxford, 85, 104

painting, 48, 61, 139
Parain, Mr, 73
Phrygian cap, 123
Paulinus, Archbishop, 15, 49, 64, 81
Pelusium, Egypt (al-Farama), 87
Penda, King, 47, 64
Pennines, 73
Pershore, 60
Peter, St, 56
  Rome, 61, 141
Petersfinger, 109, 115, 117, 120
Pevensey Castle, 89
pick, 77, 78
Picts, 27
pigs, 77
pitch-forks, 76, 80
Pitt-Rivers, General, 13
ploughs, 73–6
polychrome jewellery, 97, 132, 136–8
Portchester, 67–8, 73, 75

pommels, 111, 112, 135, 163, 165, 166
Poslingford, 140, 141
pottery, 17, 26, 33, 37, 39, 41, 48, 67, 70, 89, 98–104
    firing of, 83, 98
Pouan, 113
Prague, 123
Procopius, 27
pulpit, 61
purses, 43, 46, 164

Radford, Dr C. A. R., 69
radio carbon dating, 14, 17, 20
Rahtz, P., 24, 65, 75
Rainham, 105, 106
Ramsbury, 155
Ranulph Flambard, Bishop, 60
Reculver, cross of, 61, 149
Redwald, King, 46
reliquaries, 55, 60–1
Rheims, school of, 153, 154
Rhine, river, Germany, 27, 37
Ribbon Style, 135, 144, 166
Ringerike Style, 156, 157, 170, 171
Ringmer, 115
rings, 19, 39, 62, 98, 140
Ripon, 57
Rivet, Mr A. L. F., 69
roads, 89–90
Rochester, 84
Robert of Jumièges, Benedictional of, 152
Roman legacy, 25, 89
Roman military sites, 26
Rome, 61, 141
Rothwell, long brooches, 96
Royal I. E. VI (MS.), 150, 168
royal sites, 63–6
Rushford, 99
Ruthwell, 54, 148, 150, 168
Rupert cross, 60

St Alban 81
St Austell, 58
St Mary-at-Hill, 19
St Neots, 104
St Ninian's Isle, 141
Salin, B., 13
Sancton, pottery at, 101
Sandbach, 54
Sandtun, 76, 92
Sarre, 106, 108, 125
Sashes, nr Cookham, 84
Saxons, 26, 27, 28, 29, 34, 36–40, 47, 48
Sceaftesege, Borough of, 84
sceptre, 44, 46, 142
Schiringshal, 87
Schleswig, 37
Schola Saxonum, 141
Scilly, Isles of, 32
scourge, 58, 59–60
scramasaxes, 113–15, 166, 167
sculpture, 48, 52, 53, 147–50, 154–6
scythes, 76, 78, 80
Seaxneat, 30
settlements, archaeology of, 36–40
    rural, 63–80
    urban, 80–5
Sevington, 19
Sewerby, 35
sheep, 77–80
shields, 23, 34, 43, 115–18
ships, 35, 36, 91–2
    treasure in, 40–47
shrines, 55, 56, 60–1, 165
sickles, 76
Sigebehrt, 46–7
Sigebereht, 115, 166
Sihtric the One-Eyed, 165
Silchester, 80
silks, 21, 87, 88, 89, 92, 95
Sittingbourne, 114, 155, 166

slaves, 35, 63, 68, 87, 88
Sleaford, 100, 101, 102
Snape, 35, 91
Sophia, St, 57
South Cadbury, 84
spades, 76–7, 81
spatha, 109–12
spears, 34, 41, 118–20, 123, 166, 167
spices, 87, 88, 89
spoons, 41, 62, 132
Stamford, 99, 103, 104
standard, 44–5
Stapenhill, long brooches, 96
Stenton, Sir Frank, 21, 30, 85, 121
Stockholm, Sweden, 19
stole, 57–8, 95, 151, 170
Strickland, Sir William, 169
   brooch, 169
Strood, 125
Style I, 134–6
Style II, 134–6
Suffolk, 21, 38, 91, 99, 134, 137
Sulgrave, 66–8
Sussex, 29, 30, 38, 89
Sutton Courtenay, 69, 77, 98
Sutton Hoo, 19, 38, 40–7, 62, 91, 115, 117, 118, 121, 125, 135, 136, 137, 138, 139, 144, 163–71
Sutton, Isle of Ely, 19, 61, 157, 171
Sweden, 44
swords, 20, 34, 43, 48, 108–13
Sweyn, King, 32
symbols, of Christianity, 42, 57, 62, 123
   of Royalty, 44, 46
   of nobility, 67
   Celtic, 122–3
   Evangelists, 144, 165, 168
Symeon, of Durham, 56

Tacitus, 118
Talnotrie, 19
Taplow, 40, 106, 134, 135–6, 167
Tassilo Chalice, 19, 59, 141, 143, 169
Taylor, Dr and Mrs H. M., 50
Thetford, 23, 72, 73, 80, 82–3, 85, 99, 103, 104
tombstones, 54–5, 61, 72, 170
tools, 46, 73, 76, 78
Torksey, 99
Tournai, Belgium, 40
towns, 63, 80–84
   functions of, 85–6, 90
   planning, 83–4
trade, 17, 20, 21, 39, 84–9
   goods traded, 87–9
transport, 17, 89–92
treasuries, church, 55–8
   in ships, 40–47
tremises, 46
Trewhiddle, 19, 55, 58–60, 141, 142, 143, 147, 149, 156, 165, 169
trichinopoly, 60
Tufa (standard), 45
typology, 13–14

Uncleby, 113
Upchurch, 106
Uppland, Sweden, 43
Utrecht Psalter, 153, 154

Verulamium, 81
vessels, types of, 102
vestments, 17, 57–8
Viking art, 155–6, 157, 171
Vikings, 31–2
   encampments of, 72–3
   swords of, 112
   battle with, 126–8
villages, 63, 68–73, 90

Vortigern, 27

wagon, 90
Wallingford, 84
Wandsworth, 114
Wareham, 84, 85
Warendorf, Germany, 69
weapons, 17, 33, 41, 43, 87, 88, 108–26
Wedra, people of, 35
Wenceslaus, St, 123
Wendreda, St, 55
Wessex, 30, 31, 32, 38
Wessex, Royal House of, 31
Westly Waterless, 73
West Stow, 16, 69, 99, 165
Wheatley, 165
whetstone, 44, 45–6, 138, 164
Whitby, 102
Wight, Isle of, 26, 30, 38
Wilfred, St, 58
William the Conqueror, King, 33, 55, 124, 157
weaving, 16, 94–5
Willibald, 54
Wilton, Norfolk, 56, 136, 167
Winchester, 17, 24, 53, 62, 73, 84, 85, 95, 114, 151, 166, 167, 170 95, 114, 151, 166, 167, 170

Winchester art style, 115, 152, 153, 154, 157, 170
Wing, 164
Windsor, 114
wine, 39, 87, 88, 89
    trade, 21, 102
Witan, the, 65
Witham, river, 113, 139, 140, 145, 165, 168
Woden, 30, 118
Woodbridge, 40
wool, 77, 89, 94
Worms, Germany, 166
Wroxeter, 80
Wuffingas, 46
Wulfhere, King, 30
Wulfstan, Archbishop, 19
Wynaldum, Holland, 137, 167

Yeavering (*ad Gefrin*), 15, 23, 49, 64, 65, 66, 75
Ynglinga Saga, 35
York, 82, 87, 104, 140, 170
    military sites at, 26
    Archbishop of, 30, 86
    Mount at, 34
    cemeteries at, 37
    population estimation of, 85

More about Penguins and Pelicans

Archaeology under Water

George F. Bass

Directing the excavation of a seventh-century Byzantine ship from a twentieth-century submarine and recovering the gilded sandal of a victim from the Maya well of sacrifice at Chichen Itza are only two of the extraordinary adventures recorded in this colourful and detailed work. It ranges from Yucatan to Sweden and from Germany to the Mediterranean, from the Bronze Age to the present day.

The methods of underwater archaeology are carefully explained including search and survey techniques, draining and raising operations, salvaging artifacts and preserving underwater finds and mapping and recording underwater sites.

'Dr Bass's book, though most profitable for its clear descriptions of up-to-date method, gives also entertaining historical sketches of underwater exploration in the pre-aqualung era. Indeed, little of interest in the whole field of submarine research has escaped him . . .' – *Sir Mortimer Wheeler*

Not for sale in the U.S.A.

The Beginnings of English Society

Dorothy Whitelock

It is the aim of this book to draw together from all types of
sources evidence relating to the life and thought of the
Anglo-Saxons, from the time when they first took
possession of the Romanized province of Britain until
their unsuccessful stand for freedom at the Battle of
Hastings. It deals with their religion in heathen times, with
the ethics on which their society was based, with their
institutions, and with their standards of living. It shows
how all these things were modified by the acceptance
of the Christian faith, and how, under the influence of the
wider contacts then established, there resulted in this
outpost of the civilized world a remarkable culture. There
are also chapters on church organization and on the
achievements in literature, Latin or vernacular, and in art.
The whole account is obtained by fitting together the
actual evidence, and where, as often happens, this is
fragmentary, no attempt is made to fill the gaps with a
fancy picture which cannot be substantiated.
'The best short introduction to the study of Anglo-Saxon
history which exists in print today' – *The Times Literary
Supplement*

The Celts

Nora Chadwick

The Celtic character and imagination are still a vital part of our inheritance and whilst the purest strain is probably in Ireland, in Scotland and Wales too their influence is unmistakable.

The Celts began to grow powerful and to spread across Europe from about 1200 B.C. They were, and are, taller and fairer than the Mediterranean people. They used chariots and were fond of display, achieving superb workmanship in drinking vessels, weapons and jewellery. They started landing in Britain in about the eighth century B.C. and in the East they spread as far as Asia Minor.

In this book Nora Chadwick, a Celtic scholar of international repute, describes the rise and spread of the Celts and their arrival in the British Isles, and includes an appreciation of their religion, art, and literature in these islands. *The Celts* is a study of the people whose extraordinary individualistic and imaginative qualities have contributed so much to the world we live in today.

Rescue Archaeology

Edited by Philip A. Rahtz

Britain has an archaeological heritage of which she is justly proud. Why is it then that this heritage is inadequately preserved? Every year hundreds of sites are destroyed – motorway construction, the creation of reservoirs and deep field ploughing being only a few of the agents of irrevocable loss. The evidence for the history of man that these places could have given us is being lost for ever.

Rescue Archaeology is a collection of compelling personal statements written by some of the most eminent archaeologists of our time. They have discovered what sort of sites are being lost, who (and what) the agents of destruction are, and they propose ways in which the situation can be remedied.

The contributors to this book have one thing in common. They believe that the legacy preserved in Celtic villages, Stone Age burial grounds and Roman villas (to name but a few) can and should be rescued.

The Making of the English Landscape

W. G. Hoskins

The Making of the English Landscape can claim to be the only book to deal with the historical evolution of the English landscape as we know it. It dispels the popular belief that the pattern of the land is a result of eighteenth-century parliamentary enclosures, and attributes it instead to a much longer and more fascinating evolution. This book is a pioneer study which traces the chronological development of the English landscape from pre-Roman days to the eve of the Black Death, onwards to the Industrial Revolution and up to the present day. With the help of photographs and charts, Professor Hoskins discusses the origins of Devonshire hedgebanks and lanes, the ruined churches in Norfolk and lost villages in Lincolnshire, Somerset's marshland ditches, Cornwall's remote granite farmsteads, and the lonely pastures of upland Northamptonshire. As such, this delightful book, combining scholarship and readability, will appeal to everyone wishing to understand more and thus appreciate fully the varied loveliness of the English landscape.

'An admirable new survey. . . . He skilfully mingles the broad generalization with the tiny but relevant detail' – *Sunday Times*

'No one before has ever brought out with quite the same vividness the historical background of the country all round us' – *Guardian*

'This is one of those rare books that can produce a permanent and delightful enlargement of consciousness' – *New Statesman*

Arthur's Britain

Leslie Alcock

This remarkable book assembles all that is known or can be deduced about the most shadowy period of British history since the Roman occupation and about its legendary hero. The author of it is the archaeologist who directed the famous excavations at Cadbury Castle in Somerset, originally identified with Camelot by Leland.

Drawing evidence from both written and archaeological sources, Leslie Alcock sifts history from myth to create a convincing picture of life between the fourth and seventh centuries, when Celtic Britain was abandoned by the legions to the Picts, Scots and Anglo-Saxons.

'The amount of information . . . is terrific, but this does not prevent the book from being scholarly and readable in the highest degree . . . No one reading Mr Alcock's book could seriously doubt that an important figure called Arthur existed' – Anthony Powell

'He has produced a book which seems to a layman like myself to be authoritative, scrupulous and enlightening' – C. P. Snow

Prehistoric Societies

Grahame Clark and Stuart Piggott

'Brilliant chapters bring prehistoric man to life from the earliest times, when his tools were split pebbles, during the hundreds of centuries in which he was a food collector devising stone and bone implements for the hunt and domestic task, down to his burgeoning as a food-producer' – A. D. Lacaille in the *Tablet*

'Here are Neanderthal and Cro-Magnon, Celts and Achaeans, Iroquois and Eskimos, plentifully illustrated with rock-engravings and the tools our ancestors used in the conquest of their fellow-animals. . . . Meticulous in avoidance of speculation, it is accurate, up to date, readable and full of interest' – *Economist*

'Here is archaeology most brilliantly used for the writing of history' – Jacquetta Hawkes in the *Sunday Times*